P9-DGR-026

Body Language
QUICK & EASY

About the Author

Richard Webster is the author of fifty titles with Llewellyn, and is one of New Zealand's most prolific writers. His best-selling books include *Face Reading Quick & Easy*, *Spirit Guides and Angel Guardians*, *Miracles*, and a series of books on feng shui. MagicNZ presented him with a Lifetime Achievement Award for "excellence in writing magical literature" in 2008. His book, *Spirit and Dream Animals*, received a COVR Award in 2012. In 2013, Richard was made a Grand Master of Magic by the magicians of New Zealand. Richard has appeared on numerous TV shows including *Hard Copy* and *20:20*. His books have been translated into thirty-one languages.

Body Language
QUICK & EASY

Richard Webster

Llewellyn Publications
Woodbury, Minnesota

Body Language Quick & Easy © 2014 by Richard Webster. All rights reserved. No part of this book may be used or reproduced in any manner whatsoever, including Internet usage, without written permission from Llewellyn Publications, except in the case of brief quotations embodied in critical articles and reviews.

FIRST EDITION
First Printing, 2014

Book design by Donna Burch
Cover photo: iStockphoto.com/17934078/Neustockimages
Cover design by Kevin R. Brown
Editing by Connie Hill
Interior illustrations © Mary Ann Zapalac

Llewellyn Publishing is a registered trademark of Llewellyn Worldwide Ltd.

Library of Congress Cataloging-in-Publication Data

Webster, Richard, 1946–
  Body language quick & easy / Richard Webster. — First edition.
      pages   cm
  Includes bibliographical references and index.
  ISBN 978-0-7387-3954-0
1. Body language. I. Title. II. Title: Body language quick and easy.
  BF637.N66W437   2012
  153.6'9—dc23   2013038930

Llewellyn Worldwide Ltd. does not participate in, endorse, or have any authority or responsibility concerning private business transactions between our authors and the public.
  All mail addressed to the author is forwarded, but the publisher cannot, unless specifically instructed by the author, give out an address or phone number.
  Any Internet references contained in this work are current at publication time, but the publisher cannot guarantee that a specific location will continue to be maintained. Please refer to the publisher's website for links to authors' websites and other sources.
  Cover model(s) used for illustrative purposes only and may not endorse or represent the books subject matter.

Llewellyn Publications
A Division of Llewellyn Worldwide Ltd.
2143 Wooddale Drive
Woodbury, MN 55125-2989
www.llewellyn.com

Printed in the United States of America

Other Books by Richard Webster

This book is dedicated to the wonderful people at Llewellyn,
past and present. I'm grateful to you all for helping,
guiding, and nurturing me through 50 books.
Thank you for making it happen.

Contents

As the tongue speaketh to the ear,
so the gesture speaketh to the eye.
—KING JAMES 1

INTRODUCTION

We all communicate with each other in a variety of different ways. Talking is the most obvious one, and words, written or spoken, are extremely important. The tone of voice we use can also be interpreted. We also communicate silently with others using our bodies and facial expressions. The way we stand, move, sit, and gesture can be interpreted by others, and they decide what they think about us as a result.

You communicated with others well before you were able to say a single word. In fact, it's highly likely you controlled and influenced your parents, and other important people in your life, with your inborn skills at nonverbal communication from almost the time you were born. Consequently, you were an expert at body language well before you learned how to speak.

Imagine you're at a social gathering and meet a number of people for the first time. One of them looks over your shoulder while you're talking to him, and hardly looks at you. Another person makes good eye contact, smiles frequently, and nods his head every now and again as you're talking. Which one is interested in you? The interest of one, and the disinterest of the other, is obvious, yet it's likely neither was aware of what their body language was saying, unless one of them was being deliberately rude.

We constantly reveal information about ourselves nonverbally. Within seconds of meeting someone, we've made decisions about the person based on his or her facial expression and body language. The way he stands, holds his head, and positions his arms and legs reveals his thoughts, feelings, and emotions more clearly than any number of words.

Of course, people can make fake gestures in an attempt to conceal how they really feel. However, these are never 100 percent effective, and because of a phenomenon known as "leakage," our real feelings will still be visible to anyone who knows what to look for. Some of the elements of the gesture will be missing, as our real feelings will "leak" through the facade we're trying to create.

A common example of this is a fake smile that people display to show others they're happy. A genuine smile involves the eyes as well as the mouth. As a fake smile doesn't involve the eyes, it's easy to recognize. Like most people, I've said things such as "I'm fine," when in reality I was feeling the opposite. Despite the words, and the attempt to look as if there was no problem, my real feelings would have been visible to any student of body language. Just recently, someone assured me he had plenty of time, but while he was saying it his fingers were tapping on his desk.

This book is in two parts. The first part covers the art of body language. In this section a variety of gestures are looked at individually. The first chapter covers the many forms of nonverbal communication that can be made using the head and face. Chapters Two and Three cover the rest of the body, from the neck to the feet.

Part Two shows you how to use this information in everyday life. You'll discover how to use body language to make a good first impression, gain rapport with others, and become more likable. It contains chapters that will help you make use of nonverbal techniques in your career, in your love life, and for self-improvement. You'll also learn how to recognize the body language of people who lie or want to deceive you.

Part One
The Art of
Body Language

I speak two languages, Body and English.
—MAE WEST

chapter one

BODY LANGUAGE

Your life will change as soon as you start using the secret language of nonverbal communication consciously. It will enhance your professional and social life, and will increase your ability to get on with everyone you meet in your everyday life. You'll be able to read the body language signals of others accurately and be able to use that information to interact and communicate with everyone you deal with more effectively than ever before. You'll find the art of body language easy to learn, and it will improve your life immeasurably.

In 1967, Professor Albert Mehrabian of UCLA conducted two groundbreaking studies into verbal and nonverbal messages. They demonstrated that 55 percent of the meaning came from the person's posture, gestures, and facial expressions; 38 percent came from the pitch, tone, and speed of the person's voice; and 7 percent came from the words used. In other words, more than 90 percent of communication comes from nonverbal cues.

People have argued about the exact percentages ever since, but no matter what figures they come up with, they all agree that by far the greatest amount of communication is done silently through body language. Speech is an excellent way to convey information. However, it's our bodies that convey our moods and feelings.

Professor Mehrabian believes that the three elements of communication are verbal, vocal, and visual (the "3 Vs"). All three of these need to be congruent for the message to be believed. If, for instance, someone says, "I like you," but makes little eye contact, and has no enthusiasm in his or her voice, the person hearing those words will trust the nonverbal aspects of the communication, rather than the words.

Unfortunately, Professor Mehrabian's conclusions have been misinterpreted by people who thought the percentages related to all interpersonal communications. It's important to remember that Professor Mehrabian did not claim these percentages were valid in all person-to-person communications. His research experiments investigated communications involving feelings and attitudes.

Most people go through life completely unaware of the silent information they are receiving and sending every day. It's been proven that the most successful people in any field are those who are best at picking up and interpreting the hidden cues that everyone reveals to others unconsciously.

Some people have a natural ability at gaining rapport with others. Nelson Mandela—the anti-apartheid campaigner, statesman, and former president of South Africa—was a striking example. During his more than twenty-seven years in prison, a number of his warders became good friends because of his charisma and rapport. Nelson Mandela stayed in contact with three of them after he was released from prison.[1] Rapport is a harmonious, sympathetic, mutual understanding between two people. When you use body language appropriately, rapport occurs naturally.

Understanding body language is a vital skill that will enhance your life in many ways. As well as being able to read the hidden motivations of others, you'll become aware of the messages you're unconsciously sending to others. Some of these silent messages will be positive, but others may be negative. Once you become aware of the negative ones, you'll be able to focus on them, and gradually eliminate them.

The celebrated film actor Cary Grant (1904–1986) is an excellent example of someone who deliberately altered his body language to create the image he wanted. He said: "I pretended to be someone I wanted to be until I finally became that person."[2] This is a good technique. If you make a list of the qualities you would like to have, you can then focus on them until they become a natural part of your life. If you prefer, you can model yourself on the qualities possessed by people you admire.

A good friend of mine used to constantly touch his nose when conversing with others. This unconsciously sent out a message to others that he might not be telling the truth, when in reality it was simply a bad habit caused by childhood insecurities. Once he became aware of what he was doing, he was able to work on correcting it.

My introduction to body language came about when I spent three months working in a slaughterhouse at the age of twenty. I was there to make enough money to travel from New Zealand to the United Kingdom. At that time, in the 1960s, a large number of people from the Pacific Islands migrated to New Zealand for work opportunities. Many of them found work at the slaughterhouse. Unfortunately, the supervisors found them extremely hard to deal with. When they were corrected for doing something wrong, instead of apologizing, or looking repentant, they would look at the ground and giggle. This infuriated the supervisors, who felt the worker wasn't taking the rebuke seriously enough.

At about the same time this was occurring, the employment manager was experiencing problems with potential employees, too. When they came into his office to be interviewed, they made no eye contact, stared at the floor, and sat down immediately, even if the manager was still standing.

Management became involved, and eventually they discovered that these men were behaving in the way they had been taught back home. Looking down and giggling was a sign of embarrassment. Coming into someone's office and immediately sitting down was a sign of respect, as the person was placing himself lower than the interviewer. Looking down and making no eye contact was also a sign of respect.

Once everyone understood the body language of the Pacific Islanders the problems disappeared. Difficulties of this sort can occur whenever you're visiting a foreign country.

You should study body language if:

- You want to gain rapport with others

- You want to understand others better

- You want to create a positive impression

- You want to sell yourself in potentially difficult situations, such as a job interview

- You want to become more confident

- You want to put others at ease

- You want to get on better with your colleagues

- You want to develop closer and warmer relationships

- You want to persuade and influence others

- You want to understand other people's motivations

- You want to communicate more effectively

- You want people to respond to you more favorably

- You have any dealings with the media

- You want to progress in life

- You want to know what politicians and celebrities are really saying when they appear on TV

As you develop your body language skills, you'll notice gestures and other clues that you'd failed to see before. In addition, you'll be more aware of your own body language and be able to alter it to send out the signals you want other people to see. Making these changes will increase your effectiveness in every type of situation. While doing these, you'll be consciously aware of what you're doing. Until now, the chances are you've been doing this unconsciously.

You'll become more aware of people's everyday behavior. This is known as baseline behavior. When you know how someone acts normally, you'll immediately notice any changes in his or her nonverbal behavior. A friend of mine enjoys watching stand-up comedy, but he seldom reacts to anything the comedians say or do. A deadpan face is his baseline behavior. If he smiles during a show, it's a sign of extreme amusement. If you happened to see him in an audience, and didn't know his baseline behavior, you'd think he wasn't enjoying the show, even though he was loving every minute of it.

You'll observe all the gestures someone makes to determine what his or her body language indicates. If someone touches his nose while talking with you, he might be telling a lie, but may simply have an itch. You need to look for other body language clues to determine what the message actually is. A group of gestures is known as a "cluster."

You'll also start noticing "micro-expressions," which are brief flashes that cross the face in a fraction of a second. These leakages are almost impossible to control, and clearly tell you the person's real feelings.

You'll be able to establish and maintain good rapport with others more easily using a process known as "mirroring." This is a technique that involves matching and reflecting back some of the other person's posture and gestures.

If you're not a hermit, and have any dealings at all with other people, it's to your advantage to know everything you can about body language.

Body language, as its name indicates, is concerned with the whole body, and not solely the face. In fact, as the face is the easiest part of the body to consciously control, many people believe more accurate results can be obtained by focusing on the rest of the body. This is because it's more likely to be honest than facial expressions, which can be manipulated easily.

If you're trying to hide your true feelings, you might smile and nod your head, and think you're fooling everyone. However, your body may well be betraying you, as it's responding to your innermost thoughts and feelings.

In 1996, a group of neurophysiologists from the University of Parma made a huge breakthrough in neurology when they discovered previously unknown brain cells that they called "mirror neurons." Mirror neurons control the muscles, and consequently, how the body moves. These brain cells work not only when we perform an action, but also when it appears that someone else is going to perform an action. This is why your arms and legs sometimes move when you're focused on a football game. Sports coaches show their teams films of their previous games, as they know the countless mirror neurons will cause the players' bodies to react.

Mirror neurons explain why we see someone yawn, and then yawn ourselves. Television comedies use laughter tracks to encourage us to laugh in response. We're naturally attracted to people who are positive and full of energy, as our mirror neurons make us feel positive and full of energy, too.[3] Mirror neurons also allow us to empathize with others, as we experience an emotional response to their high and low moments.

Some people are naturally good at picking up the subtle nonverbal cues sent out by others because their mirror neurons instantly react to them. This appears to be almost intuitive, and these people naturally fit into any type of situation. However, it's a skill that anyone can learn. As your body language skills develop, you'll find your mirror neurons will start providing you with information instantly, too.

Most people go through life blissfully unaware of the nonverbal messages they're communicating everywhere they go. These people are easy to analyze, as they're not trying to conceal anything. However, some people study and use body language to help them achieve their goals. Salespeople, managers, politicians, and con artists are good examples. Other people, such as psychologists and anthropologists, also study body language for their own reasons.

Fie, fie upon her!
There's language in her eye, her cheek, her lip,
Nay, her foot speaks; her wanton spirits look out
At every joint and motive of her body.
—WILLIAM SHAKESPEARE (*TROILUS AND CRESSIDA*, ACT IV, SCENE V)

chapter two

STARTING AT THE TOP

The head and face play an extremely important role in body language. You have the ability to read the expressions on a stranger's face from as far as 150 feet away. Whenever people interact, their facial expressions change to reflect what they're discussing. Their heads also move in a variety of ways that reflect their thoughts, attitudes, and feelings. These unconscious gestures and movements are easy to observe, and the interpretations of different facial expressions are virtually the same all around the world.

In addition, when we're talking with someone we place most of our attention on his or her face. We automatically adjust our conversations according to the expressions on the person's face, as we're reading facial expressions all the time.

Recently, I happened to bump into someone I hadn't seen for many years. We had a cup of coffee together while we caught up on what we'd been doing since we'd last spent time together. He asked me how my wife was, and I told him about some of the things she was doing.

After that, I was about to ask after his wife, but didn't as I saw a brief flicker of sadness cross his face. This was a micro-expression, which is a highly distinctive gesture that comes and goes in a fraction of a second. He knew I was about to ask him about his wife, and his involuntary micro-expression anticipated my question. If I hadn't been looking at his face at that exact moment, I would have missed it. Instead of asking the question, I asked him about something else instead. Later in the conversation, he told me that he and his wife had recently separated, and he was still struggling to come to terms with it.

Some unfortunate people are unable to make involuntary facial expressions. Some stroke victims suffer from paralysis of one side of their face. Sufferers of Parkinson's disease are able to make only a limited range of involuntary facial expressions, though they can make them voluntarily when they wish.[1] The inability to make appropriate facial expressions causes many people to become reclusive and withdraw from society.

The Head

The way you hold your head can indicate interest, aggression, anger, superiority, power, submission, and boredom. If your head is held high and slightly backward, you may appear conceited and arrogant. If your head is held high and your chin thrust forward, you'll appear aggressive and confrontational.

Lowering the head can be a sign of tiredness, submission, worry, defeat, loss, or shame. It can also indicate rejection of the other person's ideas.

Head movements can indicate much more than yes and no. They can be used to emphasize or punctuate the spoken word. They can beckon someone in a situation when you may not want to call out to him or her. A brief upward movement of the head can be used as a sign of acknowledgment, and a nod can indicate agreement, approval, and encouragement.

If someone's head suddenly jerks back, it's a sign that he or she is shocked or surprised at something he or she heard or saw.

In most parts of the world a head nod is a sign of assent. However, in some parts of the world it can indicate "no." Countries where a head nod indicates "no" include Bulgaria, Serbia, Turkey, Montenegro, Slovenia, Iran, and parts of Greece.[2]

Nodding your head during a conversation encourages the speaker to continue talking. This tells the speaker that you're listening to what they're saying, and also tells him or her that you're happy to keep on listening. If you stop nodding your head, the speaker will think you've lost interest, and stop talking.

Nodding rapidly shows that the listener is aware of the urgency of the situation, or wants to speak.

A slow, prolonged nod shows that the listener doesn't fully agree with what the speaker is saying. When you nod your head in agreement with someone, start your nod by inclining your head upward, rather than downward.

Vigorous head nodding is a sign of impatience. The person doing the nodding has listened enough, and wants the speaker to stop talking.

If someone constantly nods his or her head while talking, it's a sign that the person subconsciously wants you to agree with what he or she is saying. Because of this, it can sometimes be an indication that the person is lying.

People's real feelings are revealed if they nod their head when they should be shaking it, and vice versa. If someone says, "I love you," while at the same time shaking his or her head slightly, the head shake, rather than the words, reveals the truth.

Head shaking signifies disagreement. Rapid head shaking indicates major disagreement. Every now and again, you'll come across someone who shakes his or her head slightly while talking with great enthusiasm. When this occurs, the head shake reveals the person's true feelings, no matter how enthusiastic or positive his or her words might be.

A single, quick shake of the head is a deliberate action to indicate surprise or astonishment. It appears as if the information is so amazing that the person has to shake his head to reassure himself that he's not dreaming.

People frequently clasp the back of their heads as a response to a real or imagined disaster. This is a protective gesture that provides comfort and security at a time of major stress. You can see this when watching the supporters of a team when they realize they're going to lose a game.

Clasping the Back of the Head

It's common for people to tilt their heads to one side when watching or listening to something that interests them. It's a sign of mild, polite interest, and shows they are listening. A prolonged or deeper tilt creates empathy.

Next time you become aware that you're tilting your head while talking or listening to someone, notice whether your head is tilted to the right or the left. If it's tilted to the right, you'll feel more open, as you're accessing the creative part of your brain. If your head tilts to the left, you're likely to be intellectually analyzing what's being said. A 2006 study found that tilting your head to the right makes you appear honest and dependable, and tilting your head to the left makes you appear more attractive.[3] Experiment with tilting your head to the opposite side to experience the different feelings it produces.

Women tilt their heads more frequently than men, and it can sometimes be a sign of flirtation or light-heartedness. In fact, it's not unusual for people do it deliberately when talking to someone they are sexually attracted to.

Tilting the head exposes more of the neck, and can make a woman appear vulnerable and in need of protection. It can be a sign of trust.

Because a head tilt is a sign of empathy, and is a non-threatening gesture, it can be a useful tool for men to use in the workplace. However, women should avoid tilting their heads in the workplace, as it's sometimes considered a submissive gesture.

It's a sign of criticism or disapproval if the head is tilted downward toward the other person.

Someone who is thinking or assessing something may stroke his or her chin with a thumb and forefinger. Someone with a beard may stroke or pull on it while evaluating something.

Tapping the temple or forehead with an index finger is a sign that the person who is tapping thinks the other person is crazy, or has said something so ludicrous that even the idea of it is crazy. Tapping the head is also used as a deliberate insult, suggesting that the other person doesn't possess the ability to think. Funnily enough, tapping the head can sometimes mean the opposite. If someone has said something profound, a listener might tap his or her head to show that he or she recognizes the speaker's high intelligence.

Often, when people realize they've done something stupid, they gently slap or hit themselves on their heads. This blow is normally made to the side of the face, the forehead, or the top of the head.

People often scratch their heads when they're puzzled about something. This is because their scalps start to itch when they are perplexed or confused.

Hair

The average person has 100,000 hairs on their scalp. Fair-haired people have more individual hairs on their heads than people with darker hair. People who touch, stroke, or fondle their hair subconsciously seek reassurance. When they were young children, a parent, or some other loved person, stroked their head to provide comfort and love. Stroking their hair releases stress by providing the same feelings of comfort and support.

People who twist their hair may be suffering from anxiety and stress. However, as this gesture can be habitual, the stress may have occurred long ago. An old school friend of mine used to twist his hair in the classroom whenever he felt anxious. More than fifty years later, he still does it, although now, most of the time it's nothing more than a long-entrenched habit.

Women sometimes subconsciously stroke or run their fingers through their hair to show off its length and beauty when in the company of someone they find attractive. Although this is usually done subconsciously, some women do it deliberately to increase their sexual attraction.

The Face

Our faces, particularly our eyes, are the most revealing parts of our bodies. It's been estimated that people can make more than ten thousand different facial expressions. Because the face is so revealing, people tend to believe what the face reveals. However, this is not always a good idea. It's possible to put on a "face" that reflects what we want other people to see. If you're feeling sad and downcast, for instance, you can put on a happy face that will convince some people. However, you're still likely to give yourself away through your voice and gestures.

There are times when it makes good sense to conceal your emotions. A poker player would not want other people to sense his elation at being dealt a good hand. Someone who expected to win an award, but didn't, would disguise his or her feelings, and applaud the winner. If you received some bad news over the phone, you might want to conceal your feelings if you happened to be at work, or at a social engagement. However, no matter how well you do this, people who know you well would know something was wrong. They might not be able to see it in your face, but your true feelings would reveal themselves as "leakage."

Actors are experts at manipulating their facial expressions to reveal whatever emotion is required for the role they're playing. Con men and women are another example of people who can create whatever expressions they wish, depending on the situation they're in.

Micro-Expressions

Micro-expressions are involuntary facial expressions that appear on people's faces for a fraction of a second. Because they cannot be controlled, they reveal the underlying truth about how the person is feeling. Someone may be smiling and saying how happy she is, but if a micro-expression of sadness crosses her face, her real feelings are revealed. Micro-expressions usually appear around the eyes and mouth.

The main emotions revealed by micro-expressions are happiness, sadness, fear, anger, surprise, disgust, and contempt. The expressions use all the muscles that are involved when these feelings are expressed openly, but may last only one twenty-fifth of a second.

Many people find it hard to pick up micro-expressions, which probably explains why the phenomenon was not documented until 1966.[4] A good way to practice seeing micro-expressions is to watch television footage of politicians and interviews of people who may have something to hide.

Happiness Microexpression

Happiness is indicated by a quick smile, creases at the outside corners of the eyes, and sparkling eyes.

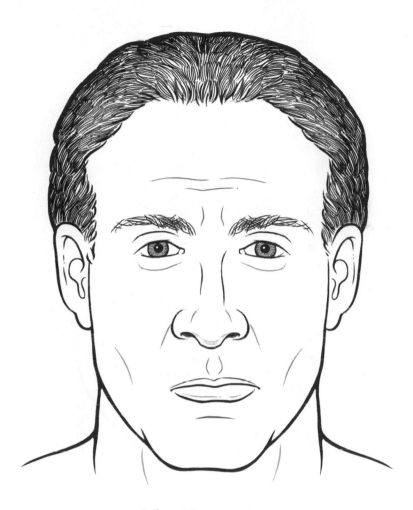

Sadness Microexpression

Sadness is shown by a creased forehead, downturned mouth, drooping eyes, and a frown.

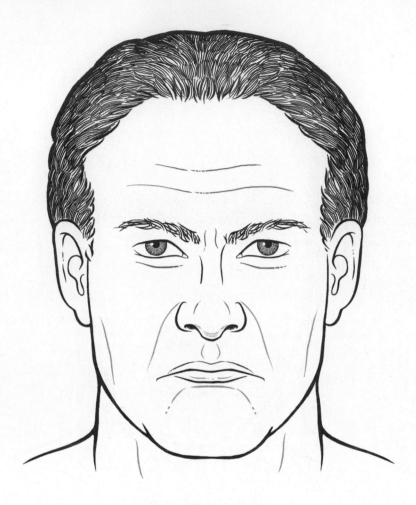

Anger Microexpression

Anger is revealed by flaring nostrils, a tightly closed mouth with narrowed lips, a creased forehead, and glaring eyes.

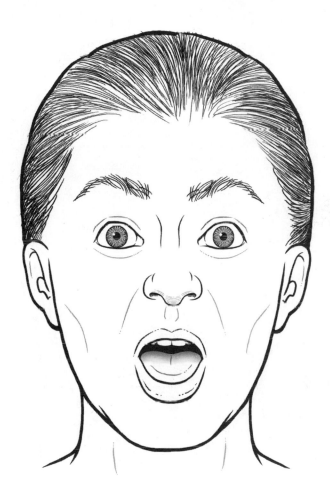

Surprise Microexpression

Surprise is indicated by widened eyes, raised eyebrows, and an open, rounded mouth.

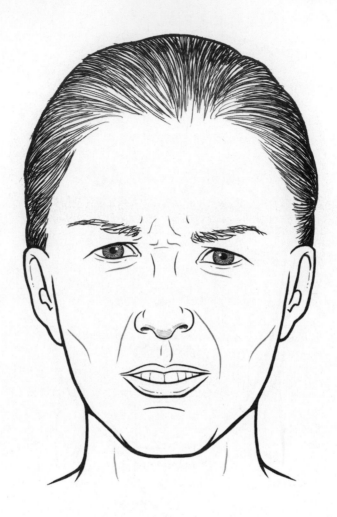

Disgust Microexpression

Disgust is revealed by a wrinkled nose, eyes narrowed, and a facial grimace.

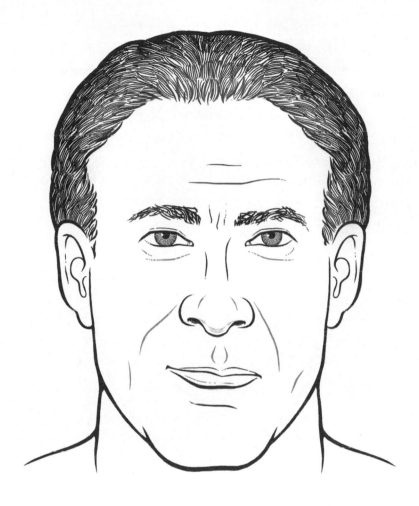

Contempt Microexpression

Contempt is shown by a curled top lip that is raised on one side of
the face, and a raised chin.

The Six Universal Expressions

In his book, *The Expression of the Emotions in Man and Animals*, published in 1872, Charles Darwin (1809–1882) claimed that there were six universal facial expressions: surprise, happiness, fear, anger, disgust, and sadness. These are the same expressions that can appear as micro-expressions on people's faces. Darwin's research was considered controversial at the time, but later investigators proved them correct. Because these emotions are easily read, people tend to mask or hide them in situations when they don't want their true feelings known. There are distinctive actions that accompany these feelings.

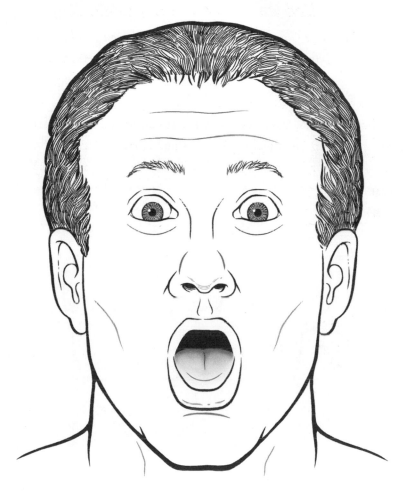

Surprise Universal Expression

Surprise

Surprise is an emotion that appears unexpectedly, and disappears quickly. Surprise is indicated by the forehead, eyebrows, eyes, mouth, and jaw. The jaw drops open, the eyebrows rise and curve, the horizontal lines on the forehead crease, and the whites of the eyes become visible. If the surprise is a pleasant one, the person is likely to smile afterward. However, if the surprise is unpleasant, the person's face is likely to reflect fear.

Happiness Universal Expression

Happiness

Happiness is indicated by the eyes, mouth, and cheeks. The lower eyelids rise slightly, and wrinkles appear beneath them. The eyes sparkle, and crow's feet may appear at the corner of the eyes. The mouth stretches outward and upward, emphasizing the lines that run from the side of the nose to outside the corners of the mouth. These lines force the cheeks to rise and swell outward. Most of the time, the mouth will open slightly to expose the upper teeth. All of this creates a warm and genuine smile.

Fear Universal Expression

Fear

Fear is indicated by the eyebrows, forehead, eyes, and mouth. Eyebrows rise and are pulled together. The lines in the forehead become more visible, and are partially creased in the center of the forehead. The eyelids rise, and expose the whites of the eyes above the iris. The lips are pulled sideways in a horizontal line. Sometimes the lips part slightly.

Anger Universal Expression

Anger

Anger is indicated by the eyebrows, eyes, mouth, and sometimes the nose. The eyebrows move down and inward, emphasizing the frown lines. The upper and lower eyelids close slightly to narrow the eyes, which glare coldly at whatever caused the anger. The lips are compressed, and turned down slightly at the corners. Sometimes the nostrils are flared.

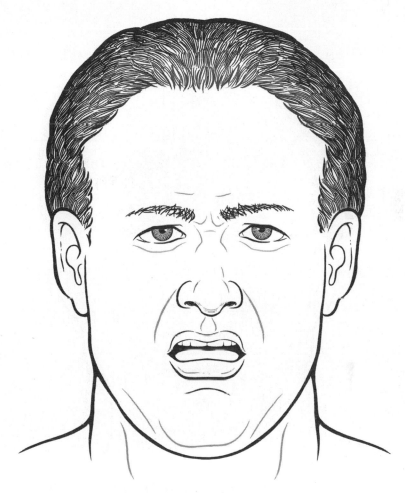

Disgust Universal Expression

Disgust

Disgust is indicated by the eyes, nose, mouth, and cheeks. The lower eyelids rise, creating fine horizontal lines immediately below the eyes. The nose wrinkles, causing the cheeks to rise. The upper lip curls and rises in the center.

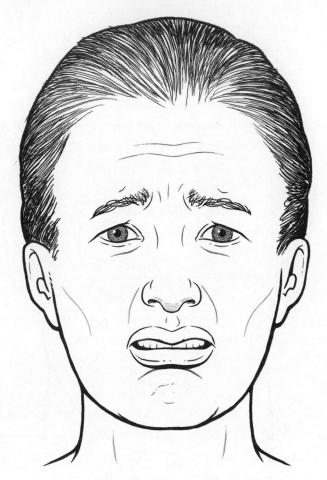

Sadness Universal Expression

Sadness

Sadness is indicated by the mouth, eyebrows, and forehead. The mouth is slack, and droops at each corner. Sometimes the lips quiver. The inner ends of the eyebrows rise, emphasizing the frown lines and the center of the horizontal lines on the forehead. The eyelids droop, and the eyes may be crying, or appear to be on the brink of tears.

The Forehead

The horizontal lines that cross the forehead rise upward when the person is surprised. They also rise when someone is pleased to see you. In this instance, the eyes widen as well.

When people suffer from stress and tension they are likely to rub their temples or foreheads to relieve the stress. Sometimes the veins become more visible to indicate the degree of stress the person is under.

Frowning

A furrowed forehead cannot be interpreted on its own, as it is caused when people are anxious, stressed, upset, angry, or focused on a task. Someone running late for an appointment is just as likely to frown as a father who is angry with a child for bringing home a bad school report. The accountant at the publishing company I worked for when I left school had an extremely pronounced single frown line caused by concentrating on figures for long periods of time.

Eyebrows

The eyebrows are extremely expressive. The four muscles that influence the eyebrows enable them to create a wide range of movements. When someone is surprised, both eyebrows rise, and the mouth usually opens. If just one eyebrow is raised, the person is skeptical about something. Some people find it impossible to raise just one eyebrow.

People automatically lower their eyebrows when they feel threatened. This is done instinctively to protect the eyes. When people find themselves in a potentially dangerous situation, their cheeks also rise to provide maximum protection for the eyes.

Eyebrows are also lowered when people feel angry or frustrated. Eyebrow lowering can be done deliberately to intimidate and control others. People who do this usually frown and tighten their mouths at the same time.

The eyebrow knit occurs when the eyebrows are raised and at the same time move toward each other, creating frown lines. This also creates horizontal lines across the forehead. The eyebrow knit is a sign of grief, anxiety, and major stress.

The eyebrow raise occurs when the eyebrows raise and move outward, flattening the frown lines and creating a series of horizontal lines on the forehead as they move. This expression is known as a "furrowed brow," and is usually considered a sign of worry. However, it can also signify wonder, surprise, delight, incredulity, and alarm.

The eyebrows are a powerful indicator of how the person views you. If someone smiles when he or she meets you, and also momentarily raises his or her eyebrows, you know that the person is interested in meeting you. The "eyebrow flash," as this is called, is involuntary, and is a sure sign that the person is pleased to see you. If, on the other hand, the person smiles, but fails to give an eyebrow flash, you'll know this person has no real interest in meeting you. People all around the world give an eyebrow flash when greeting friends.

The eyebrow flash is also used to express agreement with what someone is saying. The eyebrows also rise to express surprise or fear.

The eyebrow shrug is similar to the eyebrow flash, but the eyebrows are briefly held in a raised position before being lowered again. This is usually accompanied by both ends of the mouth turning downward. This indicates mild surprise and disapproval at something someone has said or done. It is often made as a sarcastic gesture.

A consciously made gesture is to slowly raise the eyebrows, and tilt the head to one side. This gesture nonverbally asks the other person if he or she has done something correctly or appropriately.

Eyes

Approximately 80 percent of the information we process daily comes through the eyes, making it by far the most important sense organ of the human body.

The eyes are the most revealing part of the face. We communicate more with our eyes than any other part of our bodies. This is why we have so many expressions involving the eyes. "Eyes are the windows of the soul," is a good example. "If looks could kill," "She has come hither eyes," and "He has dead eyes," are other examples. A good friend of mine writes romance novels in which the eyes of her heroes burn with desire, and the eyes of the heroines melt as a result. Young children are told to "Look me in the eye."

During his lifetime, Victor Hugo (1802–1885), the famous French novelist, was as famous for his many romantic relationships as he was for his writing. His memoirs contain many accounts of his numerous sexual encounters. They also contain a valuable clue about his success with women: "When a woman is talking to you, monsieur," he wrote, "listen to what she says with her eyes."

Even today, many people believe in the malevolent power of the "evil eye." This is the belief that an admiring or envious glance could cause ill health or even death. Children, in particular, were thought to be at risk from the evil eye, and could be affected even when the person looking at them had no malice in mind. The remedy was to say a prayer, or to touch a religious charm or protective amulet.

The eyes clearly reveal many feelings and emotions, such as trust, love, lust, surprise, hurt, impatience, anger, and confusion. The eyes are particularly useful in body language, as it's almost impossible to hide the emotions revealed in them.

The pupils of our eyes dilate when we're surprised, excited, or stimulated. This allows the brain to receive as much information as possible. The eyes will remain dilated if the surprise is positive, but will constrict in a fraction of a second if the surprise is a negative one. People are considered more attractive if their pupils are dilated.

If someone is interested in you and what you have to say, his or her pupils will dilate to reflect this. However, the lighting in a room also affects pupil dilation. If the room is very bright, the pupils will contract to counteract the harsh light. In a darkened room, the pupils will dilate to allow better vision. Consequently, you need to check the lighting in the room before deciding if someone is interested in you.

Many people believe that David Bowie, the rock superstar, has one blue eye, as well as an eye of a different color. This is not true. When he was fourteen years old, he and his friend George Underwood got into a fight over a girl. George punched David in the face, and his fingernail damaged the sphincter muscles in David's left eye. He spent four months in hospital while doctors tried to repair the damage. The result of this is that the pupil of his left eye is permanently dilated. Consequently, in bright light, the pupil of his right eye contracts, but the pupil of his left eye doesn't, making the eyes appear to be different colors. He actually has two blue eyes. David and George are still friends today.[5]

Most children are taught not to stare. I remember being told, "It's rude to stare." Consequently, we all learn to look at someone for a moment, and then, without changing expression, allow our gaze to move on. In public places, the gaze lasts for about a second. This is extended slightly in social situations. There are only two situations in which two people will stare into each other's eyes for any length of time. Lovers gaze into each other's eyes, usually unaware that they're unconsciously looking for dilated pupils. People who hate each other also stare at each other's eyes, trying to force the object of their hatred to look away. If they succeed in this, they feel psychologically stronger than their opponent. Recently, I saw two professional boxers do this on television when they were being interviewed a week before their fight.

Because the gaze is so powerful, you can show interest in someone by allowing your gaze to linger longer than what is considered acceptable in the part of the world you live in. An extended gaze can also be considered a challenge, and may be deliberately provocative. Some people stare because they wish to dominate others. However, this is impolite, and alienates people. If you're close enough to the person who is staring, you can determine if the gaze is because the person is interested in you, or if he or she is potentially hostile. If the person likes you, his or her pupils will be dilated. If the person is angry or antagonistic, the pupils will be constricted.

A blank stare is intended to be insulting, as it appears that you're looking right through the person as if he or she wasn't there. A hate stare is deliberately provocative, and is intended to intimidate the person it is directed at.

Eye Contact

Eye contact is a sign of interest. If someone at a party looked into your eyes for longer than usual, you'd think the person was interested in you, and you would probably consider him or her attractive.

Some people avoid eye contact. They may be painfully shy, or possibly have something to hide. They may have a guilty secret, or feel ashamed about something. They might feel nervous, anxious, or intimidated. They may have told a lie. People who suffer from autism and Asperger's syndrome often avoid eye contact, too. If you find it hard to look people in the eye, look at the spot between their eyebrows. The person you are looking at will not be able to tell the difference, and will assume you're giving him or her a direct gaze.

People who are shy often prefer to give a sideways glance, in preference to a direct gaze. They often look downward while doing this. Princess Diana is a good example of someone who did this. The celebrated British zoologist and author Desmond Morris called this "bold shyness." This is because, although the shy person is looking at the other person, he or she is not staring directly, and is actually demonstrating humility by looking away.

The amount of eye contact varies in different parts of the world. I remember being surprised at the amount of eye contact Parisians made while traveling on the Metro. This was because I'd just spent a year in London, where people make as little eye contact as possible on the Tube.

People in Greece enjoy looking at others, and want other people to look at them. They feel ignored if other people show no interest in them. Arabs also enjoy looking at each other, and use a great deal of eye contact while both listening and talking.[6] In Japan, a direct gaze or stare is considered rude, and direct eye contact between people of different genders is unacceptable.[7]

Good eye contact is an essential part of nonverbal communication. We tend to feel uncomfortable and distrust people who avoid looking us in the eye. Eye contact plays an important part in everyday conversation. The listener maintains more eye contact than the speaker. The listener maintains eye contact approximately 80 percent of the time, while the speaker maintains eye contact between 40 and 60 percent of the time.[8] The two people look directly into each other's eyes about thirty percent of the time. The speaker looks away from time to time while still talking. This gives him or her less sensory stimuli to deal with, and also avoids the problem of appearing to stare. After looking away for a while, he or she makes eye contact again to make sure the person is still listening. He or she will also be able to tell the level of interest and understanding by looking at the listener's eyes. As the speaker finishes, he or she will look at the listener to let him or her know it's time to respond. Looking at the speaker's eyes builds rapport and aids communication. If the listener stops looking at the speaker's eyes, he or she would quickly stop speaking, as it would be taken as a sign of boredom or disinterest.

Eye contact also lets the speaker know that you're listening to what is being said. If your eyes start wandering, the speaker will think you're not interested in what he or she is saying.

Eye contact plays an important role in establishing rapport with others. Direct eye contact is a sign of honesty, sincerity, and confidence. If you look at someone for more than a few seconds, he or she will subconsciously know that you're interested in him or her. However, it needs to be the right amount of eye contact. Too much eye contact can intimidate others, and too little eye contact makes you appear lacking in confidence, strength, and honesty. People who shift their eyes away too quickly are said to have "shifty eyes."

If you like someone, you'll look at him or her frequently. Conversely, if you don't like someone, you'll look at him or her as little as possible. This is not done consciously. It's natural to look at something that interests us, and just as natural to look away from something that is of no interest. This means that someone likes you if he or she looks at you frequently during a conversation.

Eye contact can also be used to control the listener. A speaker is likely to increase the amount of eye contact if he or she is trying to put a point forward.

The area of the person's face that you look at while talking to him or her varies according to the situation. If you meet a stranger, for instance, you look at the area enclosed by a triangle formed by the base of each eye and the top of the forehead. If you want the encounter to become more casual and friendly, you allow your gaze to encompass the area from the mouth up to the eyes. If you've met someone, and want them to know that you're interested in him or her, you can allow your eyes to move discreetly downward to the neck before quickly moving back to the person's eyes. This is a flirting gesture, which will be returned by the other person to indicate his or her interest.

Some people lower their eyes when in the presence of someone they consider important or superior to them. This is a submissive sign.

Expressions

A glare is used to silently express anger. It's usually accompanied by a frown. The person stares at the object of his or her irritation with wide-open, glaring eyes that are intended to make the other person change his or her behavior.

When people narrow their eyes, it's usually a sign of disapproval. The eyebrows lower at the same time, making the person appear angry. However, many people do this when reading or focusing intently on something.

Squinting is a sign of dislike and distrust. People tend to squint when acknowledging someone they don't like. Even though the squint may last for only a fraction of a second, it is obvious to anyone who can read the signs. People also squint when they're feeling uncomfortable or uncertain about what to do next.

Wide-open eyes are a sign of interest, especially when the eyebrows are raised at the same time. As large eyes are appealing to many people, this helps create rapport.

If the eyes are widened to the extent that the white of the eye is visible above and possibly below the iris, the person is indicating mild surprise. People reveal their disdain by narrowing their eyes.

People usually blink six to eight times a minute. If someone suddenly starts blinking rapidly, it's a sign that he or she is under stress or pressure. In extreme cases, the person can blink up to eighty times a minute. This can be a sign that the person is lying, though this would have to be confirmed by other indications. Rapid blinking simply indicates the person is uncomfortable and anxious. When former president Richard M. Nixon appeared on television to give his resignation speech, he appeared calm and relaxed. However, every now and again his eyes would blink rapidly, indicating the stress he was under. As a result of this, rapid blinking caused by extreme stress is sometimes called the "Nixon effect."

People also blink rapidly when they're on the verge of tears, and are trying to prevent that from happening.

Darting eyes are an indication that the person is feeling defensive or insecure. Most people think someone with darting eyes is lying, but this is not necessarily the case. The person might simply be nervous, or feeling anxious.

Someone who feels superior might adopt a slow blink, in which the eyes are closed for slightly longer than normal. This effectively blocks you from their sight for longer than normal, and is intended to make you aware of the power they possess (or think they possess).

A few people close their eyes for seconds at a time while talking. This enables them to formulate their thoughts without any distractions. It also enables them to temporarily escape any outside pressure or antipathy. Unfortunately, it usually comes across as an affectation. Some people find this endearing, but most people consider it annoying.

Blocking the eyes with a hand, or rubbing the eyes, is a sign that the person doesn't like what he or she is being told. When someone is given bad news, his or her eyes will close briefly in a subconscious attempt to block out the information. People also rub their eyes to avoid someone else's disapproving gaze.

Eye dipping occurs when someone wants to avoid offending someone whom he or she considers more senior or dominant. It's a deliberate, rather than a subconscious, gesture. This gesture is also common when passing a stranger in the street. When they are about eight feet apart, both will lower their eyes until they have passed each other. This indicates that the person is non-threatening. Eye dipping also occurs when someone wants to disengage themselves from a conversation. This is usually because they feel under pressure. Eye dipping is either a downward movement of the eyes, or a dipping of the head.

A sign that someone is desperate to escape a situation is rapid eye movement from side to side. This is a sign of extreme discomfort, and the eye movement makes it look as if the person is frantically looking for the nearest exit.

Winking is a potentially dangerous gesture, as it can be easily misconstrued. People who wink too frequently might be considered sleazy, and are frequently misunderstood.

A wink is sometimes intended to be a friendly gesture that encourages warmth and openness. It can also tell someone that the previous statement was not intended to be taken seriously. It can also mean, "okay," or that two people are sharing a secret or a private joke. A wink is sometimes used to soften an insult or offensive comment by silently telling the person, "I'm only joking." However, unless this is interpreted correctly, it can make the insult worse, rather than better.

Eye Movement

As well as all this, the eyes allow you to get inside the other person's mind and learn where his or her answer is coming from. The person's eye movements tell you if he or she is remembering something, visualizing it, or constructing it. You can easily demonstrate this for yourself. Stand in front of a mirror and ask, "What did my parents give me for my tenth birthday?" There's a 90 percent chance that while thinking about this question, your eyes moved upward and to your left. Here's another question: "What would the Eiffel Tower look like if it was made of wood?" To visualize this, your eyes probably went upward and to the right.

Because of this, it's possible to watch people's eye movements and know where the information they are telling you is coming from. This is extremely useful information.

The person's eye movements tell you if he or she is primarily visual, auditory, or kinesthetic. This enables you to speak to the person using the language he or she prefers.

Visual thinkers use visual phrases. Someone who is primarily visual will say things along the lines of, "I see," or "that's clear to me."

Auditory thinkers use phrases that relate to sound. Someone who is primarily an auditory thinker might say, "That sounds right," or "That strikes a chord."

Kinesthetic thinkers tend to use more emotional words. Someone who is primarily a kinesthetic thinker might say, "That feels good," or "It's a stretch, but I'm reaching for it."

People's eye movements can also be revealing. If you're talking with someone, and their eyes move downward and to the right, it's a sign that they're accessing their feelings. If their eyes move downward toward the left, they're talking to themselves. If the eyes move upward to the left, they're trying to recall something that has occurred. If the eyes move upward to the right, they're imagining something. If the eyes move to the left, they're recalling sounds. If the eyes move to the right, they're reconstructing sounds.

If you think someone may be lying, you can ask a few questions to determine where he or she is accessing the information. Once you've determined the eye movements that relate to him or her, you can start asking questions about the apparent deception. If, for example, the person should be remembering something, but accesses the area where information is being constructed, you have a right to be suspicious.

Approximately 90 percent of right-handed people use the same eye movements. Left-handed people are usually the reverse of these. However, you need to ask questions first to confirm this, as between 5 and 10 percent of people are the opposite to the norm.

If the eyes move upward and to the person's left, he or she is visually remembering something. An example might be, "What color was the front door of the house you grew up in?"

If the eyes go upward and to the person's right, he or she is visualizing something new, or seeing something familiar in a different way. An example might be, "What would a dog look like if it had huge, rubbery human lips?"

If the eyes move sideways to the person's left, he or she is remembering a sound that has been heard before. An example might be, "What does the ring tone on your cell phone sound like?"

If the eyes go sideways to the person's right, he or she is constructing sounds that have not been heard before. An example would be, "What would a mermaid's singing voice sound like?"

If the eyes go downward and to the person's left, he or she is saying something to him- or herself. An example might be, "Where did I leave my car keys?"

If the eyes go downward and to the person's right, he or she is feeling emotions or the sense of touch. An example might be, "What does it feel like to be in love?"

You can use this information to help yourself, too. If you deliberately move your eyes into the right position while asking a question, you'll be able to access the answer more quickly than if you didn't.

The Nose

Touching the nose while talking is frequently considered a sign of deception. Bill Clinton famously touched his nose twenty-six times when giving testimony to the grand jury about the Monica Lewinsky affair. This type of nose touching is called the "Pinocchio effect," as a release of chemicals created by increased stress causes the nose tissue to expand. At the same time, the nose becomes itchy.

However, there are other reasons why people touch their noses. People often tap or stroke the tip of their noses while evaluating or considering something. Consequently, this can be a sign that the person is about to make a decision.

If someone touches his or her nose while another person is speaking, it can be a sign that he or she doesn't believe what is being said.

Tapping the side of the nose is a sign that the person is busy "sniffing something out." It can also be a sign that one person gives to another to indicate that they share a secret.

A raised nose is a sign of confidence. It can also mean the person feels superior, critical, or disapproving. This gesture is usually done subconsciously, but some people deliberately raise their noses to demonstrate their perceived superiority.

It's a sign of disdain and contempt to look down the nose at someone, especially if the eyes are half closed at the same time.

If someone doesn't believe or approve of what someone is saying, he or she might briefly twist the nose to one side. This indicates that he or she "smells" something is not right. This gesture can also indicate dislike.

Flaring nostrils is a sign of arousal. The nostrils of lovers flare as they think about the delights to come. However, the nostrils also flare when someone is angry, or has made up his or her mind to do something physical. This allows as much oxygen as possible to enter the bloodstream. This is useful if the person is about to lift something heavy. However, it can also be a potentially dangerous sign that indicates the person may be about to physically attack you.

Wrinkling the nose is a gesture that most people learn in early childhood. It's a sign of disgust that is used when people don't like something they hear or see.

It can be a mild insult to place the tip of your thumb on the end of your nose, fan your fingers, and wiggle them. This gesture is usually done by children, but I have seen adults do it, too.

The Ears

Rubbing an ear between the thumb and forefinger is a sign that the person doesn't want to hear what is being said. He or she is either not interested, or doesn't believe what's being said.

It's a sign of puzzlement or doubt if someone scratches behind an ear with his or her forefinger while listening to someone talk.

It can be a sign of deception if someone caresses the back of an ear, or pulls on an ear lobe. However, in Italy, pulling on an ear lobe has a different meaning, as men there do it to indicate they've seen an attractive woman.

Rotating a finger in front of an ear is a sign that someone or something is crazy or deluded.

People sometimes cover their ears to let the speaker know they've heard enough. This might be because the subject is distressing, or they don't want to hear any more.

The Cheeks

The cheeks clearly reveal people's emotional states. Humans are the only animals who blush with shame or embarrassment. Mark Twain (1835–1910), the famous American author and humorist, wrote: "Man is the only animal that blushes. Or needs to." Blushing has erotic connotations, but in fact, most people who blush are young, innocent, naive, self-conscious, and shy. Even today, there are many "blushing brides" who fit into this category.

Blushing occurs when someone is embarrassed, shamed, or caught saying something he or she knows is wrong. People also blush when they're in the company of someone they are secretly attracted to. As blushing is totally involuntary, it clearly reveals the person's emotional state.

By the time you become aware that you're blushing, it's too late to prevent it. However, you can encourage it to fade and disappear by taking slow deep breaths.

The cheeks can also redden with rage. However, the anger is unlikely to become violent, as the person is subconsciously holding him- or herself back. The cheeks of someone about to act on his or her anger pale, as the blood is diverted away from the skin, so it can be used elsewhere. The same thing happens to someone who is terrified, as the blood leaves the skin to enable the person to flee, or stand up and fight.

Resting the cheek on one hand is a sign of fatigue, and tells other people that the person has had enough.

People sometimes playfully slap their cheeks when they've done something silly. It's a conscious gesture that simulates punishing themselves for their mistake.

A cheek kiss is a popular greeting gesture. It's useful, as it's affectionate, but has none of the sexual connotations that kissing on the mouth might create. In some places the kiss is on one side only, but it is also frequently performed by kissing one cheek, and then the other. Sometimes the first cheek may be kissed again, too.

The Mouth

The eyes find it hard to lie, but the mouth frequently sends out false information. Consequently, nonverbal messages cannot be gained by looking solely at the different expressions made by the mouth.

Our mouths create a variety of expressions every day. Over time, though, one expression will become habitual, and this can be interpreted. Even when the person changes expression, traces of this habitual expression will remain apparent.

If the mouth is loose and slack, the person will be easy to get along with, but will also be indecisive and easily influenced by others.

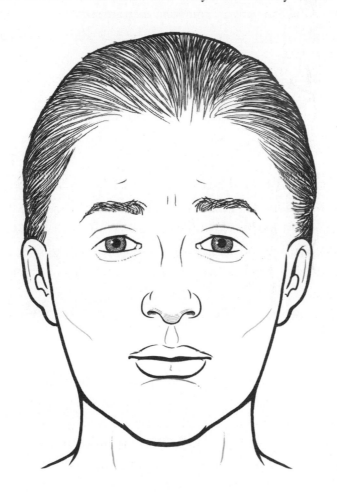

Mouth Loose and Slack

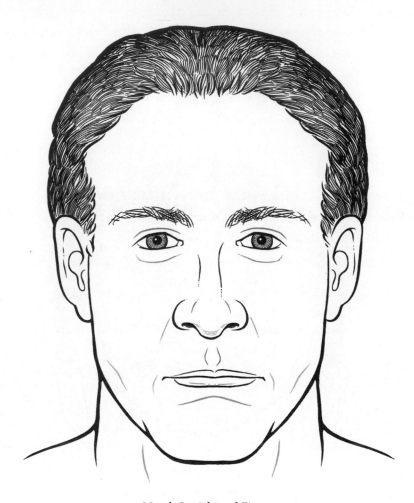

Mouth Straight and Firm

If the mouth is straight and firm, the person will be reliable, conscientious, and keep both feet firmly on the ground.

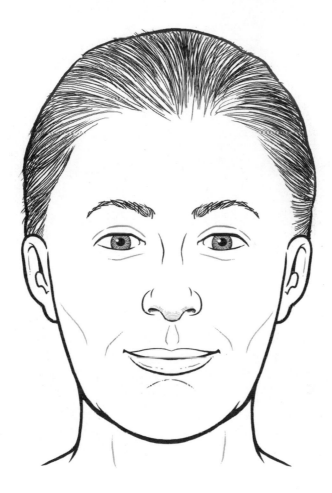

Mouth Curves Upward at Corners

If the mouth curves upward at the corners, creating a trace of a smile, the person will be easy-going, fun-loving, and easily pleased. He or she will have an optimistic approach to life.

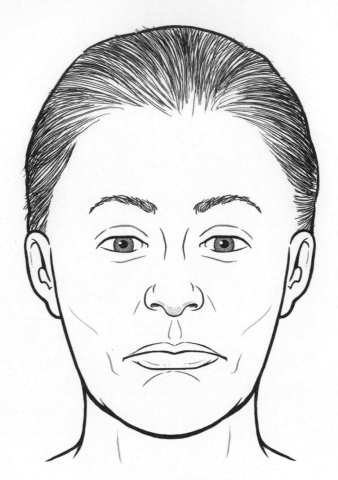

Mouth Curves Downward at Corners

If the mouth curves downward at the corners, the person will be strong-willed, unsatisfied, and difficult to please. He or she will have a pessimistic approach to life.

It's never good to cover your mouth while you're speaking. People tend to doubt your motives, and may think you're lying.

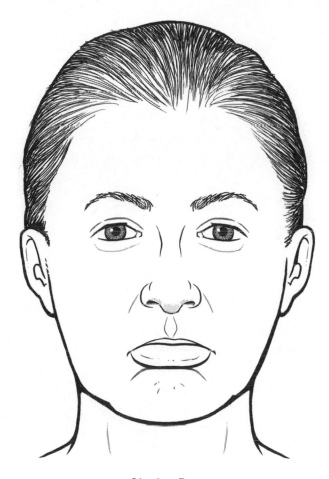

Lips in a Pout

Pouting

A pout is created by relaxing the chin and pressing the lips together. Usually, the lower lip protrudes slightly. This is a sign of irritation, annoyance, frustration, and disappointment. Interestingly, a pout can also be a sign of sexual interest.

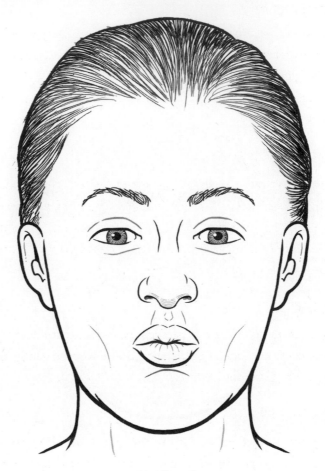

Lips Pursed

Pursing

Puckered lips are a sign of disagreement, and resistance to what is being said. It can also be a sign that the person is thinking carefully before saying anything. Pursing is an unattractive gesture, that over time can cause wrinkles around the lips. When I was in grade school, one of our teachers was called Prune Face behind her back, as she habitually pursed her lips whenever she disapproved of what her class was doing.

Lip Compression

People press their lips together into a thin, tight line when they're angry, or experiencing stress. It's a sign of major frustration, and the person is trying to hold his or her feelings in to prevent saying or doing something that might be regretted later. Tight lips are always a sign of negativity.

Lip Licking

Licking the lips may be a sign of nervousness, as people's mouths get dry when they're stressed or anxious. Sometimes it can be a sign that the person is telling a lie. It can also be a sign of flirtation. Consequently, it pays to look for other signs to confirm the meaning, rather than reading the licking of the lips alone.

Lip Biting

Biting the lower lip is a sign of shyness or embarrassment. It can also indicate anxiety and lack of confidence. Some women gently bite their lower lips as a flirtatious gesture.

Covering the Mouth

Many people cover their mouths to prevent themselves from saying something they might regret. If the fingers are spread and then placed over the mouth, the person is effectively "sieving" the words as he or she speaks. Covering the mouth can also be a sign of lying. Small children often cover their mouths after saying a lie.

Covering the mouth can also be a semi-humorous gesture. After saying something that they perhaps shouldn't have, people sometimes place a hand over their mouths, as if they were trying—too late—to prevent the words from coming out.

Many Asian people cover their mouths while smiling or laughing. This is because it's considered rude in their cultures to reveal the inside of their mouths.

Yawning

Yawning is generally considered a sign of boredom. If someone is performing a repetitive task, or experiencing a lengthy wait, he or she is likely to yawn. However, people also yawn when they're feeling tense, nervous, or facing a difficult task. These are known as stress yawns. They form a useful purpose, as they temporarily distract the person from whatever it is that's causing the anxiety.

Dominant people sometimes use a yawn when they want to assert their authority. People also yawn rather than discuss something that's causing them stress or pain.

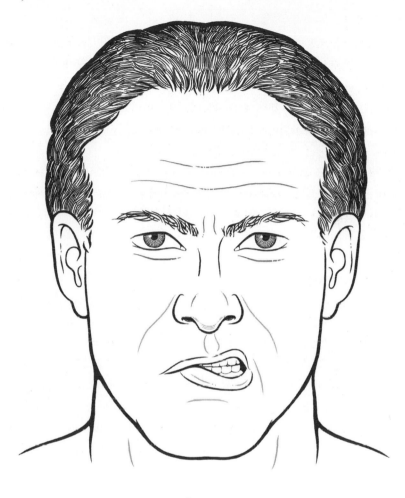

Sneer

Sneer

A sneer is a sign of scorn and contempt. It is created when the muscles on the sides of the face contract, making the corners of the lips stretch out toward the ears. The lips usually curl, also. A sneer usually lasts for just a moment, and is a sign of disrespect and disdain. However, sometimes the person chooses to keep the sneer in place to clearly reveal his or her dislike, scorn, and derision.

Sighing

It's a sign of relaxation when people sigh while exhaling. When people sigh when they're breathing in, and exhale with a "hymph" sound, it's a sign that they're stressed and upset about something. In effect, they're telling everyone around them that they're unhappy, but they're unable or unwilling to put their feelings into words.

Smiles

A smile is a sign of welcome that is known all around the world. It is the one gesture that is instantly recognized everywhere. In addition, smiling is good for you. A smile, even a forced smile, makes you feel better. Smiles release endorphins, seratonin, and natural pain killers, which make you feel happy. As a bonus, a smile reduces stress and boosts your immune system. All of us should smile much more than we do.

Even blind people can hear a smile, as they can detect it in the voices of people who are smiling. A genuine, warm smile tells others that you're friendly, honest, and easy to get along with. A genuine smile lights up the face and involves the eyes as well as the mouth. A false smile involves the mouth, but doesn't reach the eyes. An easy way to determine if a smile is genuine is to look for the crinkle of skin (crow's feet) at the corner of the eyes. If it's not apparent, the smile is not genuine.

Babies practice their smiles in the womb, up to two months before they're born. As they're totally helpless, they need to develop the muscles that create smiles to entice people to look after them.[9] Even babies produce genuine and fake smiles. An experiment performed with thirty-five ten-month-old babies showed that they could smile at a stranger without using the muscles around their eyes. However, as soon as each baby's mother came into view, he or she produced a genuine smile.[10]

Smiles are generally associated with happiness, but everyone has a variety of smiles that are used for different purposes. The most common of these is the apologetic smile that we use all day long when we accidentally interact with someone else. You'd apologize and give this smile if you accidentally bumped into someone at a train station. If you squeezed into a crowded elevator, you'd probably avoid eye contact, but would smile to effectively apologize to everyone for forcing them to stand closer together. In a busy city, the average person would use this smile dozens of times during the day. Although this all-purpose smile is a smile, it's not a genuine one.

Another smile that isn't genuine is the nervous half smile that people use when they're not feeling confident or sure of themselves. Sometimes anxiety means the smile is largely on one side of the face. I know someone who does a nervous half smile at the end of almost every sentence when he's talking. It's a sign that he feels uncomfortable, as he is not sure of himself.

Smiles are frequently used to cover up feelings and emotions. Someone who lost an important tennis tournament would smile to cover up his or her feelings while congratulating his opponent.

People who deal with the public smile to make their dealings with others more pleasant. Cabin attendants are a good example of this. However, their smiles are also intended to reassure any passengers who are afraid of flying.

There are many different types of smiles, ranging from a gentle smile with the teeth unexposed to a broad smile created in situations when someone is laughing as well as smiling.

Someone who is smiling to him- or herself gives a gentle smile with the lips closed.

When people meet, the upper incisors are visible when they smile. They also make eye contact with each other.

A broad smile occurs when people are enjoying themselves and are laughing as well as smiling. The upper and lower incisors are visible, and little direct eye contact is made.

An oblong smile occurs when people are being polite, or are pretending to have a good time. It is also used when people are holding back, and are not willing to say what they think. In this smile, the lips stretch into an oblong shape and the mouth remains closed. Consequently, this smile is sometimes known as the tight-lipped smile.

A variation of this occurs when someone grins with the lips firmly closed. This means the person is deliberately holding something back, and concealing what he or she really feels behind the smile. There is also the clamped smile, which occurs when the muscles around the mouth are tensed, creating the impression that the person was going to smile, but managed to hold it back.

Smiles of this sort can be frustrating to others, as it's impossible to tell if the person is really smiling. People who want to dominate others smile seldom. When they do, they usually use a closed-mouth smile.

The "how-do-you-do" smile is used when meeting strangers. The lips curve upward, and the mouth is opened slightly, revealing the upper incisors.

If someone is feeling anxious and fearful, he or she will often make an exaggerated smile that doesn't involve the eyes.

The politician's smile involves dropping the lower jaw while smiling broadly. From its name, you'll know that this is the smile favored by politicians and celebrities to show they're having a wonderful time. It can be a useful smile to adopt, as it looks as if you're about to laugh. Consequently, it helps others to relax and be more light-hearted.

There are many types of smiles. Paul Ekman, the American psychologist who pioneered the study of the effects emotions have on facial expression, has described fifty different types of smiles.

In 1862, Guillaume-Benjamin-Amand Duchenne de Boulogne (1806–1875), a French neurologist, conducted a series of tests to determine how fake smiles differed from genuine smiles. He electrically stimulated various facial muscles and took photographs of the different muscular contractions that were produced. He found that a fake smile was caused by the actions of the zygomatic major muscle that runs from the cheekbones to the corners of the lips. This muscle pulls the lips sideways and upward, creating a fake smile. A genuine smile is caused by the actions of the zygomatic major muscle and the orbicularis oculi muscle, which surrounds the eyes. Duchenne wrote: "The emotion of frank joy is expressed on the face by the combined contraction of the zygomaticus major muscle and the orbicularis oculi. The first obeys the will but the second is only put in play by the sweet emotions of the soul."[11] A genuine smile is sometimes called a Duchenne smile to honor his research in this field. A genuine smile is contagious. If you receive one, the chances are you'll return it, and will feel positive for some time afterward.

Many years ago, a man told me how to produce genuine smiles at any time. His solution was to think of something he found amusing. It could be a joke, a movie, a TV show, or a fun time with friends. He would choose an experience and think about it, and consequently smile or laugh, immediately before walking into a situation where he knew he would have to smile.

Research has been done on how to make smiles appear more flirtatious. It seems that smiles that take more than half a second to spread across the person's face are considered to be attractive. This is compounded if the person's head also tilts slightly toward the other person at the same time.[12]

Laughter

People laugh when they're amused. Laughter is infectious, and once one person laughs, many other people join in. People who laugh frequently are considered friendly and fun-loving. People who seldom laugh are considered uptight and humorless. Consequently, it's to your advantage to laugh more often, or at least to produce a genuine smile every now and again.

Interestingly, people also laugh when they're feeling anxious. Dr. Stanley Milgram (1933–1984), a professor at Yale University, demonstrated this with a controversial test he conducted on obedience in the 1960s. Paid volunteers were encouraged to administer electrical shocks to people who were trying to remember a list of words. Each time the student made a mistake, the volunteer had to increase the voltage. Amazingly, twenty-six of the forty volunteers were prepared to send up to 450 volts of electricity to the student, even though they could hear his cries of distress. In actuality, the students were paid actors, and received no shocks.[13]

Despite sending electrical shocks to the students, many of the volunteers felt unhappy about the situation, and about a third of them laughed and smiled when they heard the screams and cries for help. When they were asked about it afterward, none of the volunteers could explain why they had laughed and smiled. Although it appeared that they were laughing at the student's distress, the laughter was actually a nervous reaction to what they were doing.[14]

Laughter can also be used as a weapon. This occurs when someone laughs at someone, rather than with him or her. Although some people can accept this without problems, many people feel hurt and humiliated when other people laugh at them.

The Tongue

Even the tongue is interpreted in body language. If someone is stressed, for instance, the mouth will be dry, and the person will use his or her tongue to lick his lips to moisten them. When someone is focused on a particular task, he or she might poke the tip of his or her tongue into a cheek, or slightly out of the mouth. This unconscious action is soothing and helps the person concentrate on whatever it is he or she is doing.

All around the world, children, and a surprising number of adults, stick out their tongues as an insult or mildly provocative gesture.

Deep-tongue kissing is a form of nonverbal communication that needs no explanation. In the nineteenth century, many people in France enjoyed playing a kissing game called *maraichinage*. The game involved at least ten couples who swapped partners every week to indulge in deep-tongue kissing. People played this game everywhere, including churches. Not surprisingly, the clergy managed to have this game banned in 1864.[15]

Clenched Jaw

A clenched jaw is a sign of tension, frustration, or anger. Some people have permanently clenched jaws, showing that they're constantly tense, stressed, or angry. A clenched jaw is often accompanied by compressed lips. Some people clench their jaws out of habit, and in this instance, their lips are not compressed.

A clenched jaw can also be a sign of aggression. It is commonly seen in the person who is not currently speaking when two people are having a major disagreement.

A clenched jaw can also indicate the person is uncomfortable, and is feeling nervous or ill at ease.

Jaw Dropping

People's jaws tend to drop momentarily when they are surprised, disbelieving, perplexed, dismayed, or aghast. Some people drop their jaws for effect. When they do this, they keep the jaw lowered for longer than they would if the surprise was genuine. This gesture is an affectation, and can be disregarded.

Chin Jut

Jutting the chin forward is a sign that tells others to stand back or not to interfere. It's a minor act of aggression, usually performed by one male to another.

It can also be done unconsciously when someone feels angry or wronged.

Raised Chin

When the chin is deliberately raised, the nose rises with it, making it impossible to look at people without looking down the nose. This is a gesture of superiority and arrogance.

Lowered Chin

People commonly lower their chins when they're stressed or worried. When the chin is lowered, it makes the person look helpless and weak. It's a sign of hurt feelings, vulnerability, loss of confidence, and a desire to appear small. Frequently, the person's entire body droops in sympathy with the lowered chin. Consequently, the common expression "Keep your chin up" is good advice.

Chin Stroking

People who are assessing something frequently stroke their chins with their thumb and forefinger. This gesture dates back to when a beard was a sign of maturity and wisdom. Running a hand through their beards told others they were deep in thought. This gesture shows they're in the process of making a decision. If chin stroking is done during a sales pitch, the salesperson should stop trying to sell until the potential customer stops stroking his or her chin. The expressions and gestures the person makes after the chin stroking will clearly tell the salesperson whether the decision is positive or negative.

Protective Gestures

There are five important protective gestures that can be seen all around the world.

If someone covers his or her eyes with a hand or hands, he or she is consciously concealing whatever is causing the distress.

If someone covers his or her mouth, the person is protecting him- or herself from saying something that might be regretted later.

If someone covers his or her entire face with both hands, he or she is combining the first two protective gestures. With the entire face covered, the person can't see what is occurring, and is unable to make any comments about whatever is causing the distress.

If someone clasps the top of his or her head with both hands, he or she is doing it as a shield that provides psychological protection when something distressing occurs. This gesture can sometimes be seen in crowds of people at a sporting event when their team makes a mistake.

The hands may also be placed behind the person's head. This is a form of self-nurturing that goes back to when the person was a baby and had his or her head supported by his or her mother.

Deadpan Expression

A deadpan expression is one that is blank and expressionless. People sometimes adopt it to protect themselves. It's a distinctive gesture as most people's faces show some signs of animation. If you come across someone with dead eyes and a lifeless expression, you'll know that the person has given up, and is waiting for the situation to end.

Many years ago, I did a series of workshops inside a prison. Many of the prisoners had permanent deadpan expressions that they used to make themselves non-threatening and invisible. In this situation, it is an extremely useful form of protection.

People also put on deadpan expressions in crowded situations, such as buses, trains, and elevators. These people also avoid eye contact and move as little as possible.

Someone who is angry might put on a deadpan expression, so other people won't know how infuriated and annoyed he or she is.

As you can see, the head and face are extremely revealing, and provide much more information than most people would like to believe. In the next chapter we'll look at the body, from the neck to the feet, and see what we can learn from it.

Deafness has left me acutely aware of both
the duplicity that language is capable of
and the many expressions the body cannot hide.
—TERRY GALLOWAY

chapter three

FROM THE NECK DOWN

If you're feeling happy, contented, and positive about life, this will be clearly shown in your body. Your body also clearly reveals if you're unhappy, stressed, or feel threatened. Although people can often mask their feelings in their faces, few manage to successfully control the subconscious "tells" created by their bodies. They may say something, but if the body does not reflect the spoken words, they create an incongruence that can be interpreted by others. Actors are taught the basics of this at acting school, as it's important for them to be congruent. In fact, once their bodies form the right positions, they almost no longer need to act, as they'll be making the right actions automatically.

The Neck

The neck is a highly vulnerable part of the body. Consequently, it's a sign of subconscious protection when someone's hands move to that area.

If someone scratches his or her neck while you're talking, it's a sign that the person is skeptical about what you're saying, and probably doesn't believe you. Usually, the scratch is made with the index finger of the dominant hand. Sometimes, the head is tilted to one side while the person is scratching.

If someone rubs his or her neck while you're talking, it's a sign of irritation or stress. In effect, the person is saying, "you're a pain in the neck."

If someone touches his or her neck, it's a sign that the person is using the touch to release tension and calm down. Men and women differ in how they perform this gesture. Women usually touch the side of their neck, or the notch at the base of their neck. Sometimes they'll fondle a necklace to achieve the same effect. Men tend to grasp the front of the throat close to the Adam's apple.

If someone's hands suddenly clasp the throat, it's a sign that he or she has seen or heard something shocking and distressing.

It's a sign of embarrassment or stress if someone's Adam's apple gives an involuntary jump. It could mean the person has heard something he or she doesn't agree with. This movement of the Adam's apple is difficult to control, making it a useful guide to the person's real feelings.

Shoulders

The shoulders are easily read, as they're extremely mobile. They can be raised, lowered, shrugged, hunched, squared, and rounded. Someone who is feeling comfortable and relaxed will have lowered shoulders, as they are free of tension, and his or her arms will be loose. If the same person becomes anxious or alarmed, his or her shoulders will rise and move forward. If the situation is serious enough, this person will also lower their head into their shoulders. Hunched shoulders may be a result of bad posture. If this is not the cause, the person may be feeling resigned and overwhelmed.

Tension gathers across the shoulders. Tense shoulders are raised slightly, and the head is held slightly lower than usual. This can be a sign of anxiety or worry. If the person also averts his or her gaze, it's a sign that he or she wants to be left alone. Someone who suffers from stress and tension every day at work will have constantly tense shoulders, which can produce headaches and back pain.

People shrug their shoulders for different reasons. It can demonstrate indifference or embarrassment, be part of an apology, or be an indication that the person has had enough and is giving up. Usually the shrug is a deliberate gesture, but it can also be done subconsciously, and reveal what the person is really thinking, regardless of what he or she might be saying.

When someone raises his or her shoulders in apology, he or she usually looks upward or downward to avoid the other person's gaze, and holds out both hands palms upward in a traditional gesture of appeasement.

Shoulders are held evenly most of the time. If one shoulder is held noticeably higher than the other one, it's a sign that the person is evaluating something. It could almost be said that he or she is "weighing" the pros and cons of the proposition.

In the Western world, squared shoulders are a sign of honesty and integrity. However, if the squareness appears exaggerated, it's often a sign of insecurity. The person has deliberately straightened his back and squared his shoulders in an attempt to appear confident.

Someone who keeps his or her shoulders squared all the time will be rigid, uptight, and inflexible. Someone with shoulders that are both squared and relaxed will be confident and feel in total control of his or her life.

Slumped shoulders are often a sign of anxiety, sadness, and even depression. They can also indicate low self-esteem, lack of confidence, and insecurity. Nowadays, however, it's more likely that the hunched shoulders are caused by the person spending too much time on the computer. If you become aware that your shoulders are hunched, roll them forward and backward a few times to eliminate the buildup of stress in the shoulder muscles. People sometimes droop their shoulders deliberately to express exasperation. This gesture is often accompanied by a sigh, and a slight shaking of the head.

Bringing the shoulders forward and hugging them is a comforting gesture that provides feelings of safety and security. It subliminally reminds people of how they hugged their parents when they were small children.

Someone who crosses his arms, with the fingers exposed, and shoulders pushed forward is aggressive, angry, and spoiling for a fight.

When you're talking face to face with someone, angle your shoulders to parallel those of the person you're talking to. When you do this, the other person subliminally senses that you're interested in what is being said. Squaring your shoulders makes you appear bigger and more confident.

Chest

It's possible to tell people's emotional state by observing how they hold their chests. Someone who has just received an award may have a chest that's "puffed out with pride." This can also be an assertive gesture. Someone who has just experienced a major setback may reveal the opposite, and display rounded shoulders and a concave chest.

When men feel comfortable and happy, they're likely to unbutton their jackets to reveal more of their chests.

Placing a hand on one's chest to indicate loyalty dates back to ancient Greece. Two thousand years ago, the heart was believed to be the center of a person's being. Consequently, placing a hand on the heart meant much more than the emotions and feelings we think about today. This is why speakers touch their chests when they want to refer to themselves.

Arms

The arms are a safe place to touch on someone else's body. If we want to attract someone's attention, we'd be likely to gently tap him or her on the arm. If we were helping a stranger cross a road, we'd take him or her by the arm. If we were helping an elderly person get up from a chair, we'd hold his or her elbow. If we were guiding someone to a specific place, we'd place a gentle hand on his or her arm. In most places, two people can link arms and walk together, without anyone considering it anything other than friendliness. The arms are considered a safe, nonsexual part of the body.

People who feel self-conscious are never sure what to do with their arms and hands. They may hide their hands in trouser pockets, clasp or touch hands in front of themselves, or perhaps do as the Duke of Edinburgh does, and clasp them behind their backs. They usually find it hard to let their hands and arms hang down at their sides.

This is unfortunate, as people who stand with their legs apart, and arms hanging loosely down at their sides, portray confidence. These people are instinctively trusted by others, as the position is calming, solid, and symmetrical.

Crossed Arms

Crossed arms look defensive, and make people appear closed-minded and negative. This is one thing about body language that most people know. However, someone with crossed arms is not necessarily using them as a barrier. Although it may look defensive, people cross their arms for many reasons. They might be cold, there may be no arm rests, or they may simply feel comfortable hugging themselves. It may even be a habit. People tend to mirror others. Consequently, if one person in a group crosses his or her arms, others are likely to subconsciously imitate the gesture.

However, if you're trying to sell something to someone who has his or her arms folded, you want to make sure that the person is not being defensive and putting up a barrier to your pitch. You can make them break this position by handing them something to look at.

There are also variations of the crossed arms. A former boss of mine always placed one hand on the negotiating table, and then placed his other hand on top of the first hand. This created a barrier that the people he was dealing with would have to get through if they were to make a sale. Another technique he used when standing was to grasp one arm with his other hand. I have no idea if he did these motions deliberately, but in effect, these were disguised versions of the folded arms, and served the same purpose whenever he was negotiating.

You can be sure that the crossed arms are a barrier if you can detect muscle tension in the person's fingers. If, for instance, someone is squeezing their upper arms, it's a sign that they are suffering from tension or stress.

Arm Sweep

Sweeping gestures are used to emphasize the person's enthusiasm for what he or she is saying. They serve as a form of punctuation.

If the sweep starts away from the body and finishes with the hands touching, or almost touching, the chest, it's a sign that the person is accepting responsibility. It silently says, "I'm in charge," or "I'll do it."

Arm Punctuation

The arms are frequently used to emphasize what the person is saying. The gestures can be small or large, and sometimes look as if the person is a conductor directing an orchestra. Generally speaking, the more passionate the person is about the subject, the more animated his or her hands and arms become. It's possible to increase the energy of a meeting by increasing the size and frequency of your gestures. However, you need to be careful not to overdo this, as it can make you appear less convincing, and less authoritative.

Forearm Jerk

Listeners also use arm movements. They might, for instance, rotate the arm to encourage the speaker to hurry up and make his point.

Arms can also be used to convey insults. One of the best known of these gestures, all around the world, is the forearm jerk. One hand holds the other arm just above the elbow while the forearm acts as a phallic symbol and makes a jerking gesture.

Hands

The hands are second only to the face in their ability to send nonverbal messages to others. They're certainly used more for this purpose than any other part of the body. People almost always move their hands unconsciously when they're talking. These movements help put emphasis on different words, and clearly reveal the person's feelings. Even people who were born blind use their hands to help them talk.

The hands are also used to help people calm down when they're anxious or stressed. Touching any part of the body can be calming, but most people stroke, rub, or touch the face or neck. As excessive hand movement can be a sign of anxiety, you may want to think about what to do with your hands in that particular situation. You might decide to place your hands on your lap, either separate or interlocked, if you're sitting, and by your sides if you're standing.

The Palms

When the palms are exposed and facing upward, the person is sending out a message of honesty and openness. It can also be a pleading gesture.

When the palms face downward, the person is expressing dominance and a desire to control. A parent telling children to quiet down is likely to use this gesture, with the hands moving slightly upward and downward.

When the hands are held parallel with the palms facing each other and the fingers open, the person is feeling confident and in control.

Palms facing forward is the international sign for "stop." Speakers use it when informing a talkative audience that it's time to pay attention. School teachers use it all the time. It can also be used in conversation when the speaker wants to finish what he or she has to say. In this case, it tells the other person to hear him out, and wait his turn.

A friend of mine rubs his palms together whenever he hears something that excites or motivates him.

Palms sweat only when the person is suffering from stress. On a hot summer's day, other parts of the body will sweat, but the palms will remain dry. When someone becomes anxious, their palms will gradually become damp, and this will steadily increase until the anxiety passes. I've seen people with small puddles of water in the center of their palms, caused by anxiety and stress.

Steepled Fingers

Steepled Fingers

When all the fingers of one hand touch the same fingers on the other hand, you create what is known as a steeple. It's a sign of confidence, authority, control, and power. It shows that the person feels totally at ease, and is confident in the thoughts he or she is expressing. However, it can be considered arrogant, and should be used sparingly.

If the person steeples his or her fingers while you're talking, it's a sign that he or she is thinking carefully about what you're saying. Although you're talking, this person still feels he or she is in control.

Thumbs Up

The thumbs-up gesture is a sign that everything's fine, or that the person it is being shown to has done well. It also means "okay." Bill Clinton uses the thumbs-up gesture frequently.

In most of the Western world, hitchhikers use this gesture to get a ride. However, this gesture is considered rude in Nigeria, and you could be assaulted if you used it there.[1]

Thumb Pointing

Pointing at someone with your thumb is usually a sign of contempt and lack of respect. It can be used to ridicule someone. Women, in particular, tend to dislike this gesture.

Hand Chop

When the side of the person's dominant hand hits the palm of the other hand in a chopping motion, he or she is emphasizing a point strongly. It is usually used when the person is defending his or her position. In extreme cases, the chopping movement is used to emphasize each word. The chop is often seen as an aggressive action, and should be used sparingly, if at all.

Finger Point

Pointing your index finger at someone is usually considered rude and offensive. It normally occurs when someone wants to assert his or her authority or control. A gentler way of pointing is to use the whole hand, in either a vertical or palm-up position.

The finger point can be a useful gesture when it's aimed away from the other person. It can be used to mark off the different points the speaker is making, and helps to maintain interest. If you're going through a contract with someone, you might point at each clause in turn to emphasize them.

One-Finger Salute

The "finger" or "one-finger salute" has been used as an insulting gesture for at least two thousand years. The ancient Romans called it *digitus impudicus*, which means "impudent digit." In the West, the middle finger points upward, symbolizing a phallus. The other fingers are held down, and the back of the fist faces the other person. The upraised finger can be displayed motionless, or alternatively jerked sharply upward.

In other parts of the world, variations of "the finger" can be seen. In the Middle East, the hand is held palm downward, parallel to the ground. The fingers are splayed and the middle finger points downward. In Brazil, the entire forearm acts as the phallus. It is jerked upward to give a powerful insult known as "the banana."

The Fig Leaf

The fig leaf occurs when the hands are folded over each other and are held in front of the lower body. In men it looks as if they're protecting their genitals. Women also use this gesture at times. It's a protective gesture that shows the person is feeling vulnerable, insecure, or apprehensive. It's a sign of emotional pain. This gesture can also be made by holding something else in front of the lower body, such as a briefcase or handbag.

When I was a teenager, a girl who lived nearby always held her schoolbag, or something else, in this position. Although, at the time, I had no idea what the gesture meant, I was fascinated by her posture, as every time I saw her she was holding something in the fig leaf position. I hope she managed to overcome her adolescent fears.

Hands Behind the Back

The Duke of Edinburgh usually holds his hands behind his back when he's out in public. This gesture signifies dominance, and tells other people to keep their distance. When I was in high school, several teachers used to walk around the playground with their hands held behind their backs. As well as dominance, this can also be a sign that the person is thinking about something and doesn't want to be interrupted.

Holding the hands behind the back is an interesting gesture, as it hides the hands. It's generally better to keep your hands visible and use them in your interactions with others. Hands are extremely expressive and help your spoken words. Your hands also, of course, allow you to touch others at appropriate moments.

Hand and Finger Rubbing

Stress and anxiety are revealed when someone rubs his or her hands and fingers. Rubbing the hands together, or stroking the fingers of one hand against the palm of the other are both signs of nervousness and tension. It's a sign of stress if the fingers of both hands are interlaced and then rubbed together. Wringing the hands is another common sign of tension and stress.

Clenched Fist

A clenched fist is a sign of hidden anger. It shows that, despite other positive signs such as a smile, the person is unhappy and probably dislikes the person he or she is with.

A clenched fist can also indicate insecurity. When the fingers are balled up inside the palm, the hand looks smaller, which subconsciously makes the person feel smaller, too.

Handshake

The tradition of shaking hands is extremely old, and depictions of people shaking hands have been found that date back to at least 2500 BCE. Although no one knows how it evolved, it's thought to be a gesture of peace, as the two people shake with their right hands, which are obviously empty.

Shaking hands is a conscious, rather than unconscious, act. Consequently, it's not strictly part of body language. However, as handshakes are extremely revealing, it's worth mentioning them.

When you meet someone for the first time, you're likely to shake hands. It's a sign of openness, trust, and geniality. If you want to make a good impression, you'll ensure your hands are dry and you'll smile and look the person in the eye as you shake hands. If you want to appear submissive, you may avoid eye contact, or perhaps glance briefly into the person's eyes. Whenever possible, stand up to shake hands.

A normal handshake involves both people's hands clasping in a vertical position. The two people should be directly facing each other, making eye contact, and smiling. The palms of both hands should contact each other. Press firmly, but not too hard. Start talking before releasing the other person's hand. When your hands separate, continue looking at the other person for a second or two. Many people look down at this moment, displaying a submissive gesture. When you look away, look to one side or the other, rather than down.

If you want to demonstrate openness and a willingness to talk, you can offer your hand with the palm turned up slightly. This is the total opposite of the dominant handshake.

People who want to appear dominant or superior hold their hand palm down to gain a very real "upper hand." Not long ago, a friend of mine was planning to buy a new bed. I recommended a store that had sold us a good bed a few years earlier. My friend went in but immediately walked out again, as the salesman had given him a dominant handshake. It's always unpleasant to receive a handshake of this sort, and the amount of business that must be lost by people who use it would be incalculable. If you want to get on with others, you should never use it.

If you wish, there are remedies you can use if someone gives you a dominant handshake. However, the person will know exactly what you're doing and might take offense. You can hold your hand out in a vertical position and wait for the other person to shake it. Sometimes this person will then try to turn your hand palm-up while shaking it. When this occurs, you should have no hesitation in resisting it. You can immediately place your other hand over the person's hand, sandwiching his or her hand between yours. Alternatively, you can step forward into the person's personal body space, and twist the hands into a vertical position as you do so. If you feel the situation demands it, you might even twist the hands until your hand is on top. At a course I gave on body language many years ago, one of the students showed us how he dealt with a dominant handshake. As soon as the shake was made, he raised his hand, taking the other person's with it, and kissed the back of the dominant person's hand. I haven't been brave enough to try that method, but it would certainly be effective.

The most unusual handshake I've ever received was when I met Kreskin, the famous psychic entertainer. He has an extremely vigorous handshake that raises and lowers the hands at least a foot in each direction. I shook his hand almost forty years ago, and I have never forgotten it.

People shake hands in many ways. Everyone has experienced the bone cruncher and the dead fish. The bone cruncher involves an excessive amount of pressure. This type of handshake is usually made by aggressive people who want to use their physical strength to control and dominate others. However, it can also be done unwittingly by people who are excited to meet you, or are simply unaware of their own strength.

The dead fish handshake occurs when you're offered a totally limp hand. This type of handshake is often used by people who are submissive and lacking in confidence. It always appears weak and ineffectual. However, many people who shake hands repeatedly, or perform delicate work with their fingers, use this type of handshake to protect their hands. If you were a concert pianist would you risk giving a firm grip handshake to a bone cruncher? The managing director of the first company I worked for after leaving school was tall, athletic, and charismatic. His staff regularly talked about his handshake, as he used the dead fish, something that appeared totally out of character. However, he controlled a large business with thousands of employees around the world. Whenever he visited different subsidiaries, he made a point of shaking everyone's hand. This meant that he frequently shook hundreds of hands a day, and he'd adopted the dead fish to protect his hands.

There's another important reason why some people give a weak hand-shake. People who suffer from arthritis, for instance, might give a weak handshake because they find it painful to shake hands at all. A friend of mine who has arthritis has developed an interesting handshake using only his thumb. He offers his thumb, and after a few moments of hesitation, the other person usually links his thumb to it, and they shake thumbs.

The politician's handshake occurs when one person envelops the other person's hand with both of his or hers. This is supposed to make you like the person, or at least believe he or she likes you. However, most people who receive it don't like it. If you want to emphasize the fact that you like someone, or are thrilled to meet them, gently touch the person's arm or elbow with your other hand while shaking hands.

Both ex-presidents George W. Bush and Bill Clinton use their other hand to touch the people they are shaking hands with. Mr. Bush touches the person's shoulder or elbow, and Bill Clinton uses his left hand to pull the person closer to him. Both of these are warmer, and are re-ceived more positively, than the usual political handshake.

Handshakes can last for different lengths of time, depending on where you happen to be. In most business settings, the handshake lasts about three seconds, and the hand is pumped two to four times. In Japan, people will continue shaking your hand until you gently extri-cate it.

There are times when you'll initiate the handshake, and also occa-sions when you'll wait for the other person to hold his or her hand out first. If you're the host or hostess, you'll hold out your hand to welcome your guests. If you've been forced into a meeting involving a dispute of some kind, it would probably be inappropriate to offer a handshake when you arrived. However, if the problem was resolved, you'd prob-ably shake hands at the end of the meeting.

On any occasions when you're uncertain who should initiate the handshake, extend your hand first. This sends out a message of confidence and sincerity. In social situations, it's a friendly gesture to extend your hand first whenever possible.

It's perfectly appropriate for a man to initiate a handshake with a woman in a business environment. However, as many men are unsure what to do in this sort of situation, it's a good idea for the woman to initiate the handshake to ease what could be an awkward moment.

People who are anxious or nervous often have sweaty palms. This creates an unpleasant first impression, as no one likes to clasp a damp hand. The remedy for this is to keep your hands out of your pockets, and to hold them open to allow any perspiration to fade away naturally. If sweaty hands is a problem, keep a clean handkerchief in your pocket, and insert your hand to dry it on the handkerchief shortly before shaking hands. If there isn't enough time for this, you might have to discreetly wipe your hands against your clothing to avoid giving a damp handshake.

It's been estimated that the average person shakes hands almost 15,000 times in the course of his or her life. In 2010, when Chevrolet, the car manufacturer, instituted a five-year promise to ensure that all their deals were conducted appropriately, they asked Professor Geoffrey Beattie, Head of Psychological Services at the University of Manchester, to create a formula for the perfect handshake. This formula involves a firm squeeze done with a cool, dry palm, approximately three shakes, good eye contact, a genuine smile, and appropriate words, all done in two to three seconds.[2]

When meeting someone for the first time, it's a good idea to repeat the person's name while shaking his or her hand. Everyone likes hearing their own name, and doing this helps you remember it. Many people fail to remember a name because they don't hear it properly in the first place. As you have to hear the person's name before repeating it, doing this ensures that you have an opportunity to both hear and say the person's name. This dramatically increases your chances of re-membering it.

Handshaking is less popular today than it has been in the past, and young people are using other forms of greetings, such as a hug, an air kiss, a high five, a fist bump, a half wave, or a peace sign.

Hugging has become much more popular in recent years, and is a friendly, casual way to greet friends. It's a strong sign of love and acceptance. When men hug other men, they make contact with their arms and upper bodies.

The air kiss usually involves the two people's right cheeks touching, and a kiss is made in the air next to the person's face. Sometimes a kissing sound is made, but it's not essential.

The high five originated in the 1970s as an alternative to the handshake. It's a friendly gesture that symbolizes happiness, high spirits, and power. The high five is made by the two people raising their hand, with fingers open, above their head and slapping each other's hand.

The fist bump, known as a dap, originated during the Vietnam War and was a recognition that the two people were on the same side. A dap between two friends is a gentle tap of the fists, with the hand held horizontally, and the curled fingers of each fist facing downward. With people who do not know each other well, the dap is often performed with the fist held vertically, with the thumb on top. Barack and Michelle Obama helped increase the popularity of the dap when images of them doing a horizontal dap was shown on the news during his 2008 presidential campaign.

The half wave occurs when the right hand is raised and moved slightly from side to side. It is used only in casual situations, and is normally done when the two people are too far away from each other to hug or kiss.

The peace sign is a V gesture made by the first and second fingers, with the palm facing outward. It's an internationally recognized peace sign as long as the palm faces outward. It's an offensive gesture in the

United Kingdom, Ireland, Australia, and New Zealand when the gesture is done with the palm facing inward.

You need to be aware that some people do not shake hands for religious reasons. Orthodox Jews, for instance, do not touch people of the opposite gender. Some Muslims believe they should not touch anyone they are not related to. If someone from the Shia sect touches a non-Muslim, he or she becomes spiritually impure and has to receive ritual purification. The inability to touch others can create problems, especially in hospitals where physical contact is an essential part of a patient's treatment. In the United Kingdom, a Muslim asylum seeker was awarded a prize for his voluntary work, but lost it after refusing to shake a woman's hand.[3]

Hands on Hips

Hands placed firmly on the hips is often a sign of defiance. Standing with your hands on your hips makes you appear larger. Consequently, this gesture is often used to express confidence, and assert authority and power. It can also be a sign that the person is unwilling to cooperate.

As this gesture makes the person look larger, they also appear more threatening. Arms akimbo, which is what this hands-on-hips posture is called, is often used by people in authority to express their dominance over others.

It is also an anti-social gesture that is used by people who want to repel others, at least for a few moments. If two people are deep in conversation, for instance, one of them may stand with arms akimbo to send out a silent message telling other people to keep away. If someone is standing on his or her own with arms akimbo, it's a sign that he or she wants to be left alone.

A half akimbo gesture is used when the person wants to demonstrate his or her distance from people on one side. If the person wants to distance him- or herself from the people on the left, for instance, he or she will place the left hand on the hip, and allow the right hand to remain by the side so he or she can continue to associate with the people on the right.

Men place their hands on their hips with the fingers pointing toward their genitals. Women usually do the opposite, and have the thumb facing forward and the fingers pointing toward the buttocks. However, many women place their hands on their hips in the same way that men do. Both ways look natural on a woman. However, a man can appear effeminate if he places his hands on his hips with the thumb forward and his fingers pointing toward his buttocks.

Like every gesture, standing with arms akimbo needs to be read in context. If it's a hot, humid day, someone might stand like this in an effort to cool down. In this situation, the gesture has nothing to do with isolation or aggression.

Legs

The legs and feet are extremely honest, and seldom lie. They reveal confidence, nervousness, happiness, and even timidity and shyness. They can be flirtatious, or act as barrier. They also show when someone wants to leave.

Standing

When people stand with their feet about shoulder length apart they are relaxed and comfortable. When the feet are placed wider apart than this, the person is making him- or herself appear larger, and therefore seem more dominant and powerful. If the feet are placed less than shoulder width apart, or even together, the person is feeling defensive and is subconsciously making him- or herself appear smaller. If the person stands with his or her legs so close together that the knees are touching, it's a sign of timidity and insecurity.

If someone stands with the weight evenly distributed on both feet, he or she will be well balanced and receptive to new ideas. If the person constantly shifts the weight from one foot to the other, he or she will be feeling uncomfortable and ill at ease. Rocking to and fro, from one foot to the other, can be a calming action if the person finds him- or herself in a stressful situation.

If the person stands with the weight on one hip, and the other leg forward, this leg can be used to point toward whatever interests him or her.

Crossing legs while standing is often a protective gesture that provides the person with a barrier to fend off unwelcome ideas or people. As this is an unstable position, it can sometimes be a submissive gesture. It can also indicate lack of confidence.

Walking

People walk in different ways, but what they do while they're walking can be read and interpreted.

People who stride take long steps, and walk using plenty of energy. Someone who strides is motivated and goal-oriented. This person knows where he or she is going, and will not be diverted or sidetracked.

People who swagger strut, rather than walk, with their heads erect and chests thrown out, nonverbally telling everyone how conceited they are. Someone who swaggers is telling the world that he has a huge ego, and is not going to let anyone stand in his or her way.

People who stroll walk in a leisurely fashion. Someone who strolls has plenty of time, and is enjoying the walk. An amble is similar to a stroll, but involves brief pauses, changes of direction, and time to admire the view. This person is relaxed, and has peace of mind. He or she is quietly confident that everything will work out well.

A plod is a slow, steady, heavy-footed walk. Each foot is placed down forcefully. This can be a sign that the person is tired, down-hearted, or depressed. However, this doesn't apply if the person is walking up a steep incline, as most people plod when walking uphill for any length of time.

People who shuffle walk in a shambling manner without raising their feet. Someone who shuffles is likely to be old, in poor health, or depressed. If the person is depressed, the chances are the shoulders will be drooped, the head will be lowered, and he or she will find it hard to make eye contact with others. This person will walk more slowly than he or she usually does.

Someone who rushes is likely to be stressed, and trying to do too many things at once.

Someone who walks steadily, with shoulders back and head straight, is reliable, conscientious, and disciplined.

Someone who walks with both hands in his or her pockets is likely to be an introvert. However, this can also indicate someone who is angry or upset, and is deliberately concealing his or her feelings. If someone has both hands in the pockets and is also walking slowly, the chances are he or she is experiencing rejection and could be depressed.

The interpretation is quite different if only one hand is in the pocket. This is a sign that the person is feeling upbeat, carefree, and relaxed.

Someone who walks with folded arms is feeling defensive and is protecting him- or herself. If the arms are folded tightly, the person is feeling anxious or apprehensive.

Someone who is deep in thought is likely to walk slowly, while looking downward. The hands might be in the pockets, or moving slightly. The facial expression is also thoughtful, and may include a frown, or chin stroking.

Sitting

Sitting with the legs apart is comfortable for most people. However, this is also a symbolically vulnerable position as it provides no protection for the genitals. Consequently, few people sit like this in public, unless they're feeling particularly confident. Most people who sit with their legs apart in public use their hands, or an object, such as a book or a briefcase, to conceal the genital area.

This is a popular position in situations where the lower half of the body is partially or fully hidden. At a dinner party, for instance, many of the people sitting around the table will sit with their legs apart, as it's a comfortable position.

Most of the time, sitting with the legs apart is done only when the person is with family or close friends. It's possible to look at a group of people and tell how relaxed and at ease they are by seeing how many of them are sitting with their legs wide apart.

This pose is rarely done by women, but is common with dominant men. It effectively makes them look larger, as they take up more space.

Leg Pump

A leg pump occurs when someone, often a man, raises and lowers the knee and heel of one foot in a pumping action. Sometimes this gesture is done with both legs simultaneously. The leg pump is a sign that this person is happy and contented. This gesture is not often used by women, but is frequently used by men. However, you shouldn't read a leg pump on its own, as it can also be an indication of nervousness.

Feet

The feet have been called the most honest part of the body. This is because people pay attention to their expressions and body language, but forget to consider the messages that are clearly revealed by the feet.

Because people turn toward things they like, and turn away from things they don't, the feet provide valuable clues that can be interpreted. Most of the time, people aren't aware of the direction their feet are facing, yet when they want to leave, one or both feet will move to point toward the door.

In the same way, when two people meet, their feet may not initially point toward the other person. However, as the conversation develops, without either person being consciously aware of it, their feet will gradually change position until they are pointing toward each other. If this doesn't happen, there is either a lack of rapport, or one or both of them might be in a hurry to go elsewhere. If a third person happens to join them, you can tell if they want to include him or her in the conversation by watching their feet. The foot nearest the new arrival should turn slightly in his or her direction as a sign that the person is welcome to join in the conversation. Hopefully, both people will make this unconscious gesture.

This also applies when people are sitting down. If both feet are flat on the floor, at least one of them should be pointing toward the other person to show that a connection has been made.

It's possible to see who's being included and who's being excluded by looking at the feet of a group of people. If everyone's feet are pointing toward the center of the group, everyone is in harmony.

Rapid Leg and Foot Movement

There are two possibilities when someone starts jiggling their legs and feet. It can be a sign of impatience, and a desire for the other person to speed the conversation up. Repetitive tapping of a foot is a sign of boredom, and is a sign that the person is subconsciously marking time.

It can also be a sign of happiness. When something good happens, people often jiggle their legs and feet. Even when they walk, it's possible to detect a bounce in their step.

Frequent movements of the feet are a sign of discomfort and unease. Sometimes the feet are crossed and one foot jiggles. The feet can be flat on the floor, and one of them taps the floor impatiently. Sometimes the anxiety is partially concealed by raising and lowering the toes. Frequent foot movements can also be a sign that the person is lying. This is especially the case if the feet are partially hidden by a table or desk.

Pointing Feet

It's a sign that someone wants to leave if his or her feet move to point away from you. Interestingly, the foot indicates the direction he or she will leave in.

This gesture can also be found in people who can't leave a conversation or meeting, but would much rather not be there.

If someone sits down with his or her feet pointing inward, it's a sign of subservience, and a lack of confidence. People sometimes adopt this stance when they feel humiliated and hurt. If the person sits down with his or her feet pointing outward, he or she feels confident and in control of the situation.

Leg Positioning

It's become something of a joke to say that someone has a "wide stance," but it's actually a sign of territorial possession, that shows the person is confident and in control. It makes the person appear larger, and conveys authority, dominance, and—sometimes—aggression. Consequently, it's sometimes possible to defuse a potentially difficult situation by closing your legs slightly to symbolically reduce your size.

Strange as it may seen, this stance is often seen in people who want to exert their dominance, but are in fact uncertain of their ability to do so. Once they've achieved their goal, the need to stand with legs wide apart disappears.

Legs Crossed

Someone who is standing with his or her legs crossed at the ankles is relaxed and comfortable. However, if the legs are tense and rigid, the crossed legs are serving as a barrier. In extreme cases, the arms will be crossed also, and this shows the person is completely closed off from whatever is being proposed.

People often sit with their legs crossed. Crossing the legs at the ankles is a common position. In a casual setting it's common for people to stretch their legs out and cross them at the ankles. This shows they're relaxed and comfortable.

Crossing the legs at the knee can be done for comfort, especially by women, but it can also be a protective gesture to keep people at a distance.

Crossing one leg at the knee and resting the ankle on the other knee is a masculine gesture. It indicates confidence, and because it takes up room it demonstrates dominance and a sense of being in control.

If you are sitting next to someone who has crossed his or her legs, you can tell if the person is interested in what you have to say by looking at the direction the raised leg is pointing in. If it's pointing toward you, the person is interested. Conversely, if the raised leg is pointing away from you, the person is using his or her thigh to subconsciously block you off.

Friends are likely to mirror each other's leg positions. In a situation where one person is more senior or dominant than the other, he or she is likely to cross his or her legs in a different way to the subordinate to emphasize his or her perceived superiority.

If you sit with your legs locked tightly at the ankles, or alternatively wrap your legs around the two front legs of the chair you're sitting in, it shows that you're uncomfortable, and you're revealing your anxiety and worry to others. The more tightly crossed the legs are, the more defensive the person will be.

Many women draw attention to their legs by sitting cross-legged with the top leg pressed against the lower leg. It makes the skin appear toned and youthful. This is an extremely feminine gesture that most men find appealing.

If someone who is sitting with his or her legs crossed is bored, he or she will reveal this by repeatedly kicking the upper leg. The leg doesn't move far before returning to its starting position, ready for another slight kick.

Rubbing the Thighs

Some people rub their thighs with their hands when they feel anxious or stressed. The more the stress increases, the more vigorous and intense this gesture will become.

Fidgeting Feet

Fidgeting feet are a sign of impatience. If someone taps a foot rhythmically, it's a sign that he or she wants to leave.

Personal Space

We all exist inside an invisible bubble of personal space that we psychologically consider ours. Only family and close friends can come inside it without making us feel uncomfortable. The amount of personal space varies from place to place, and person to person. My father-in-law was a farmer, and needed a great deal of personal space. People who have grown up in large cities need much less personal space. People traveling on a crowded bus, train, or elevator have to temporarily give up some of their personal space. However, this is regained as quickly as possible when people get off and give the remaining passengers more room. Most people cope with this sort of situation by turning their heads away and avoiding eye contact. If they have a newspaper, handbag, or briefcase, they'll likely to use this as a barrier.

Most people feel uncomfortable if someone they don't know well enters their personal space. This can be done deliberately, if someone is trying to dominate someone else. Recently, I saw a manager stand right behind a secretary to see what she was typing. He was literally breathing down her neck, and I felt sorry for her as he was completely unaware of her obvious discomfort.

However, it is more usual for this to happen unwittingly when someone who needs little personal space is talking to someone who needs more. You can sometimes see this at cocktail parties when one person keeps backing away from someone who keeps encroaching into his or her personal space.

If you want to get along well with others, it's important that you don't enter other people's personal space. Everyone knows the feeling of discomfort when someone invades their personal space. If you're talking to someone, and they take a step back, don't immediately step forward, as you've probably made them feel uncomfortable by unintentionally entering their personal space.

Two or three times a week I meet friends at a local coffee bar. The tables are small, yet we all keep our cups, saucers, and other implements in our section of the table. This is another example of personal space. If, after I finished my drink, I pushed my cup more than halfway across the table, I'd make the person opposite me feel uncomfortable, as I'd be invading his personal space.

Intimate space extends approximately eighteen inches from the body. The only people who can enter this area without causing discomfort are family members, lovers, young children, and close friends.

Personal distance starts about an arm's length, or eighteen inches, from the body and extends up to four feet from the body. This is the distance we stand away from friends and colleagues when conversing with them.

Social distance extends from about four feet to eight feet from the body. This is the distance we stand away from acquaintances and strangers. It is also the traditional distance between someone sitting behind his or her desk and the person sitting in the chair on the opposite side. Nowadays, that distance is often contracted as more and more people work in cubicles rather than offices.

There is also a public space which is used when addressing groups of people. This space extends from about eight feet away from the body.

The study of personal space is called *proxemics*, a term coined by Dr. Edward T. Hall (1914–2009), the cultural anthropologist, in 1963. He derived the word from *proximity*, which means closeness or nearness. In his book *The Hidden Dimension*, he discusses the different spaces people need to maintain around themselves.

Body Positions

If two people are standing and talking to each other, the most comfortable position for them to stand is at an approximately 120-degree angle to each other. When three people converse, the angle is about 60 degrees. Almost everyone does this automatically. Now that you know it, you'll see examples of this everywhere you go.

It can appear dominating, and possibly confrontational, to stand directly in front of someone while talking.

Remember, no matter how hard you try, you will not achieve rapport with everyone. We're all different, and every now and again, you'll come across someone who just doesn't like you. Continue to be pleasant to him or her, but focus your attention on the people who appreciate you for all the wonderful qualities you have.

Now that you're aware of how revealing the human body actually is, we'll look at clusters, or groups of postures. We need to do this, as it's difficult to read a single gesture accurately. However, when it's seen as part of a group of postures, the overall picture is easier to read and understand.

Part Two

How to Interpret Body Language

A blur of blinks, taps, jiggles, pivots and shifts ...
the body language of a man wishing urgently to be elsewhere.
—EDWARD R. MURROW

chapter four

HOW TO INTERPRET A COMBINATION OF TRAITS

Sometimes it's possible to know someone's feelings at a glance, but whenever you can, observe the person for a while before making a decision. By doing this, you'll be able to observe when someone's body language changes. Not every action has a meaning. Someone might rub his nose because it's itchy, or change position to make himself more comfortable. However, if he touched his nose or became fidgety every time you asked him a question, you might have reason to doubt his honesty. It's easy to make mistakes in interpreting body language.

The most important changes occur when someone moves from an open position to a closed one, or vice versa. If someone sits down, crosses his arms and legs, and makes little eye contact, you can safely assume that he's nervous and is trying to protect himself. If, after a few minutes, he uncrosses his arms and legs, starts showing animation in his face, and makes better eye contact, you can assume that he's feeling more relaxed and is open to what you have to say.

Conversely, if someone appears relaxed and open, but then changes to a more closed body language, you'll know that he or she has probably become defensive for some reason.

A salesperson, for instance, will become more confident when his prospect uncrosses his arms, as he knows that a barrier has been removed. If the prospect then starts to slowly stroke his chin, the salesperson knows the prospect is considering the offer. If he then smiles and nods his head, the salesperson has probably made the sale.

In this instance, uncrossing the arms was not enough to tell the salesperson that the prospect was going to buy. The arms might have been folded because the client was cold, or perhaps he crossed his arms out of habit. He may even have wanted to show off his brand new Rolex. However, the cluster of gestures clearly told the salesman of the prospect's intentions.

A few weeks ago, the manager of a bookstore told me that the book they'd ordered for me hadn't arrived. As he told me this, his head made a very slight jerking motion, his Adam's apple started bobbing up and down, he started blinking rapidly, and one hand moved up to rub an ear. He was telling me the truth when he said the book hadn't arrived, but I'm pretty sure, after observing his body language, that he'd completely forgotten to order it.

Submissive gestures often occur in clusters. People who are feeling nervous might, for instance, might cover their mouths, make poor eye contact, fidget, not know what to do with their hands, and adopt a slumped posture.

As well as observing this in other people, you should also pay attention to the body language signals you're sending out to others. If you're feeling slightly nervous, and are holding your hands in front of you as a form of subconscious protection, try putting your arms down to your sides, to display a more open body language. This might feel awkward at first, but if you continue doing it, it will become your new reality and people will see you as being open and friendly. Be aware that your clasped hands might not be the only sign of leakage. If you're nervous, you should also take a few deep breaths, focus on making good eye contact, smile genuinely, and listen to what is being said. With practice, you'll forget about your nervousness, and be able to relax and enjoy yourself in a situation that you previously found difficult.

If need be, you could also repeat positive thoughts to yourself, as your thoughts control your actions. If, for instance, you said, "I'm confident, calm, and relaxed in every type of situation," your posture would change to reflect that.

In everyday interactions you should try to exhibit as open a posture as possible, to ensure pleasant, cooperative, and smooth dealings with others.

Body Language Assumptions

A friend of mine is a smoker. Most people he deals with are unaware of this, as he smokes outdoors, dry cleans his clothes regularly, and eats dozens of breath mints every day. Because of his smoking habit, he becomes anxious whenever he finds himself in a lengthy meeting, as he's desperate to get outside for a cigarette. Someone observing him, without knowing this, would assume that something in the meeting had created the anxiety.

Many years ago, a client asked me if something was wrong, as I'd suddenly become anxious. The anxiety had nothing to do with the meeting I was in. I'd suddenly remembered I was supposed to be at another appointment. I'm glad he asked me the question, as otherwise he would have misinterpreted my change in body language. He was also good enough to reschedule the meeting, so I could race to the other appointment.

Scratching is another common example. People tend to scratch themselves when under stress, although most of the time people scratch because they have an itch. A friend of mine suffers from psoriasis, which is affected by the slightest bit of stress or tension. In her case, she scratches frequently anyway, but scratches much more when she's under pressure.

People make assumptions based on people's posture, too. A good friend of mine was an army officer for more than twenty-five years. He marches, rather than walks, and has an erect, upright posture. Everywhere he goes, people assume he's honest, conscientious, reliable, and has a position of authority.

I have another friend who slouches. His posture is sloppy, and people assume he's unambitious and lazy. In fact, he's just as conscientious, honest, and reliable as my other friend, and has a more senior position.

The posture of both friends is a result of habit. After twenty-five years in the army, my military friend would probably find it hard to adopt a more relaxed looking posture. The army dedicated many hours to teaching him how to stiffen his back, and he'd probably have to invest just as much time to lose his naturally dominant posture. Similarly, my slouching friend has held himself like that for as long as I can remember. Both could change their postures if they really wanted to, but it would take considerable effort.

The posture of one is telling the world exactly who he is, but the other is unconsciously giving a misleading impression that must affect the way people look at him when they first meet.

Another friend is something of a chameleon. His whole body language changes according to the group of people he happens to be with. After being fascinated with this for a long time, I asked him if he was deliberately mirroring the people he happened to be with. He was amazed, as he had no idea he was doing it. He automatically mirrored people everywhere he went. This ensured he fitted in with the people he was talking to, and was comfortable in all types of situations. However, someone who judged him based on a quick observation of his body language would probably make totally wrong assumptions about him.

At some stage, my friend must have decided, probably uncon-sciously, that the best way to fit in was to adjust his body language to match the people he was with. It was his way of dealing with poten-tially difficult or stress-producing situations.

A relative of mine is fidgety, and can't sit still for any length of time. I don't like sitting next to him in a movie, as he constantly fidgets in his seat, even though he's engrossed in the movie. When he stands, he's likely to jiggle one leg. People who meet him for the first time as-sume he's nervous and impatient. He's neither of these. He's simply a fidgeter.

Because of all of this, you need to observe someone for a while to determine their normal behavior. Only then will you be able to notice any deviations from this, and be in a position to act on the information.

The ability to get on with others is an extremely useful skill. If two people have equal abilities, but one possesses good people skills and the other one doesn't, it's not hard to predict which one will do better in life. The person with people skills will have many more friends. He or she will find life easier, smoother, and richer in every possible way. Fortunately, knowledge of body language can help us gain rapport with others. That is the subject of the next chapter.

The single biggest problem in communication
is the illusion that it has taken place.
—GEORGE BERNARD SHAW

chapter five

HOW TO MAKE A GOOD IMPRESSION

Rapport occurs when two people are in a state of "at oneness" with each other. It's a sympathetic, supportive, harmonious connection that occurs when two people relate well to each other. Good friends experience this type of feeling whenever they spend time together. The word *rapport* comes from an old French word, *rapporter*, which means "to carry something back." This means that what one person sends out, the other sends back.

One of my sons is extremely keen on sports. Whenever he meets another sports enthusiast, they're almost immediately in a state of rapport, because his enthusiasm for the game is obvious, and he receives the same energy from the other person.

Building rapport with clients is an important sales tool, which is why salespeople are taught techniques to help them gain rapport with potential clients. Rapport is essential in all areas of life. Some years ago, we changed veterinarians as we had no rapport with the one we had been using. When I replaced my car, I visited a number of dealerships until I found a salesperson I felt happy with. My daughter moved her daughters from one ballet school to another because she couldn't gain rapport with the owner of the first school. Without rapport, there's no relationship.

Gaining rapport is essential in the workforce. If you work in a company of any size, you'll have good rapport with some of the other workers, but may have little or no rapport with others. However, if you really want to, you can increase your rapport with everyone. Improving your working relationships will make your days more pleasant, and much less stressful.

There are a number of things you can do to help gain rapport with others.

Eye Contact

Good eye contact is important in all face-to-face encounters. However, you don't want to make the other person feel uneasy by staring into his or her eyes for long periods. A lengthy, unblinking stare is a good way to intimidate people. Conversely, poor eye contact is considered a sign of lack of interest in the meeting.

I learned this the hard way. In the early 1980s, I spent one week a month reading palms in shopping malls. This was extremely popular, and I always had a lengthy line of people waiting for a reading. I found that I could squeeze more readings in by virtually ignoring the person's face and devoting all my attention to his or her palm. However, this didn't work, as people considered my apparent lack of interest in them as a person insulting and rude. As soon as I discovered that, I started making good eye contact again.

Facial Expressions

To gain rapport with others, ensure that your facial expressions are positive. People enjoy spending time with happy, positive people.

Would you rather spend time with someone who looked happy, or someone with a scowl on his or her face?

Smile

A warm, genuine smile is one of the best ways to gain rapport with someone else. It immediately makes you appear more attractive to the other person, who will almost always smile back. It's an unusual person who doesn't respond to a genuine smile.

Head Nods

When the other person is talking, nod your head whenever you find yourself agreeing with him or her. This is an encouraging and friendly gesture that increases the likelihood of rapport, as it shows you are in agreement with each other.

Relaxed Posture

A relaxed posture makes you appear unselfconscious and easy to get along with. When you feel relaxed, the people who are with you will also relax.

Mirroring

Mirroring the other person's posture should be done gradually, and you probably won't want to mirror the other person exactly. Mirroring should be done subtly. If it's not, it might appear to the other person that you're mimicking him or her, and this destroys any chance of gaining rapport.

A good way to start is to mirror just one part of the other person's posture. If he or she is resting a hand on a table, you might do the same. You might even find that you've mirrored the other person unconsciously, and already have a hand resting on the table. After a minute or two, you might mirror something else the person is doing.

You'll know you've succeeded if, after a while, you change your own posture and notice the other person has changed to mirror you.

Many people feel self-conscious and embarrassed when they first start to consciously mirror someone else. This is because they fear the other person will notice what they're doing. This is unlikely to occur, especially if it is done slowly and cautiously. No one has ever accused me of deliberately copying their actions. This is not to say that it has never been noticed. I've certainly noticed people mirroring me, and have never commented on it. In a way, it's a compliment, as the person is doing it as he or she wants to gain rapport. If someone ever commented on it to me, I'd simply apologize, and explain that I was doing the mirroring as I wanted to get to know him or her better, and gaining rapport was a good way to do that. However, I doubt if I'll ever need to do that, as all of us are subconsciously mirroring other people all the time. Consequently, if you mirror someone deliberately, it's extremely unlikely that anyone will notice it.

Once you've gained rapport, you're in a position to gradually lead the person in whatever direction you wish. Not long ago, I had lunch with a friend who had been laid off, and was feeling depressed about his lack of success in finding another job. He was on his way to a job interview, and wasn't feeling at all confident about it. When I first sat down, I mirrored his slumped posture, and even mirrored the depressed tone in his voice. As we talked about his efforts to find work, I slowly adjusted my posture, and allowed some enthusiasm to get into my voice. He responded to this by sitting more upright, and started speaking more positively about his work prospects. By the time we parted, he was feeling reasonably positive about the interview. He didn't get that job, but was offered a position a few days later.

Attention

Giving the other person your full, undivided attention is one of the best ways to gain rapport. You need to listen carefully to what the other person is saying, and allow him or her to finish speaking before responding. Interrupting somcone before he or she has finished speaking is not a good way to create rapport.

Make the other person feel he or she is the most important person in the world to you. If you do that, the other person will never forget you.

Self-Disclosure

Self-disclosure occurs when you tell someone something about yourself that helps them understand you. Many people find it hard to open up and reveal some of themselves to others, but it plays an important role in gaining rapport. If you reveal something of yourself, the other person is likely to reveal something about his or her life, too. You can share virtually anything, including your thoughts, feelings, aspirations, successes, failures, likes, and dislikes.

Start by sharing something trivial and unimportant. As you get to know the other person, you can gradually reveal more of yourself. He or she will respond by sharing more information about him- or herself. The results of this will be shown in your body language, as your posture will become more open, and you'll become more comfortable spending time with the other person.

Self-disclosure plays a role in all relationships, but is especially important in romantic relationships. In fact, a romantic relationship could not last for long if one person disclosed information about him- or herself, and the other person didn't.

Gaining rapport is not hard to do. All you're doing is helping the other person feel comfortable spending time with you. Once you reach that stage, you can forget about body language, as you'll both be subconsciously doing all the right things.

You'll come across people who will not allow you to gain rapport with them, no matter what you do. You have two choices in these cases.

You might decide it's not worth the effort, and walk away. Alternatively, you can persist until you gain some measure of rapport.

At times, over the years, I've refused to admit defeat and have kept working at people until I won them over. One of these people works at a post office I visit regularly. She never smiles, and is unpleasant to everyone. She shouldn't be doing a job that involves dealing with the public. It took me years to win her over. Now, when she sees me waiting in line, she smiles and waves, and we have a pleasant chat while she's serving me. I have yet to see her smile at any other customer.

If you're working or regularly dealing with someone like this, you have no choice but to remain pleasant and continue your efforts until he or she allows you in. Even in these cases, the techniques in this chapter will smooth the process by enabling you to get on with these people at a superficial level until you make a breakthrough.

Likability

Your body language tells people a great deal about you before you've even met them. We all make assumptions about people within seconds of meeting them, and it can be hard to change people's initial impressions. This is why people make comments along the lines of: "From the moment I met her ..." and "He didn't fool me for a minute ..."

Your likability plays a huge part in your happiness and success in life. Very few people manage to survive without interacting with others. If you make the people you deal with feel good about themselves, they're going to like you and enjoy spending time with you. Your relationships with others are vitally important in every area of your life.

Some years ago, I was taken out for dinner by someone I hadn't met before. He was a tall, imposing man, with a loud voice. I'll call him Tom. The restaurant was a large one, and was about half full when we arrived. Tom walked right past the hostess, found a table he liked, sat down, and yelled at her, "We're sitting here! Okay?" As the waiter didn't arrive instantly, he called out again sixty seconds later: "Where's our waiter?"

The waiter rushed to our table with menus, and hovered close by, apparently concerned about Tom's loud voice and intimidating posture. He took our food and drink order, and went away to attend to it. The drinks arrived quickly, but the meal took longer than Tom thought it should. Our waiter was taking orders at another table, but this didn't bother Tom. He called to him, demanding to know when we'd get our meals. The waiter promised to find out, and came back a minute later to tell us our meals would be ready in about two minutes. "I want them here in sixty seconds!" Tom bellowed.

Our meals arrived about a minute later, and Tom ate his with relish. I wasn't quite so keen to eat mine. I worked for a while as a waiter when I was a student, and know what sometimes happens to the food of people who are difficult to deal with.

Tom obviously wasn't concerned about being liked. The tip he left was so small that I said I needed to go to the bathroom, and gave the waiter a proper tip on my way back.

Apparently, Tom is like this everywhere he goes. He likes bossing people around and appears to enjoy being disliked. I'm sure he receives bad service everywhere he goes because of his attitude. He's an extremely intelligent man who has done reasonably well in his career. However, he's never achieved the success he desired, and I'm not surprised, as I'm convinced his arrogance, ego, and rudeness held him back.

If he'd learned a few basic skills about dealing with others, plus some body language, I'm sure he'd have been much more successful, considerably less stressed, and would have a circle of good friends.

There's a saying that goes: "People do business with people they like." It's not enough to be good at your job. You also need to be likable.

When I was in my late twenties, a small business I owned failed, and I found a position as a sales representative. The owner of the company wasn't the slightest bit concerned that I knew nothing whatsoever about the products I was to sell. I discovered later that he employed me mainly because he thought his customers would like me. He was an aggressive man who'd worked hard and built up a successful business. However, he'd made more than his share of enemies along the way, and everywhere I went his clients told me how much they disliked him. Fortunately, he had some good agencies, and I was able to do a good job for him. When we called on clients together, people described us as "good cop, bad cop." Rather than try to become likable himself, this man chose to employ people who he thought would be liked.

How to Become More Likable

It's not hard to make a good impression. The essential requirements are appearance, expression, a genuine smile (with an eyebrow flash), good eye contact, and the ability to listen. People with these qualities are often described as charismatic. Some people are fortunate enough to do all the right things naturally. However, anyone can improve their skills in these areas if they want to.

Years ago, I had the pleasure of meeting Uri Geller, the Israeli psychic. He's the most charismatic person I've ever met. While I was with him, he gave me his full, undivided attention, as if I was the most important person in the world. I liked him from the moment I met him and still have positive feelings about that meeting, even though it was twenty years ago. When I met him again, a year or two later, he greeted me like an old friend. He is a remarkable, extremely charismatic man.

Good grooming plays an important role in your appearance. It also makes you feel more confident. Keep a pleasant expression on your face, and smile readily.

Make good eye contact, and let people detect the true feelings that are revealed in your eyes. You can't conceal the emotions that are expressed in your eyes, and people will be able to read love, sympathy, worry, and happiness in them.

Laugh readily, when it's appropriate. Allow your emotions to be revealed in your face and body language. Lean toward the person you're speaking to. All of these convey warmth and friendliness.

The ability to listen—really listen—is vitally important. I'm sure you, like everyone else, have had the experience of talking to someone and noticed he or she was looking over your shoulder, rather than focusing on what you were saying. People can tell in your eyes when you're looking at them, but are paying no attention to what they're saying.

Remember to nod your head every now and again while listening. This encourages the person to continue talking. A slight head tilt and an open posture also encourage good communication.

It shouldn't be the case, but the ability to truly listen is rare, and people who do it are always considered likable.

Almost everyone has a cell phone nowadays. They're a useful tool, but do nothing to aid face-to-face communication. When you meet someone for a casual cup of coffee, turn your cell phone on to silent for half an hour, and keep it out of sight. I know you might get an important call, but you've agreed to have coffee with this person, and he or she deserves your full attention. You can attend to the call afterward. By doing this, you can devote your attention to the conversation, and will be able to contribute and listen fully, rather than be distracted by your phone. If you forget to put your phone on silent, silence it if it rings. The person you are with will appreciate this, as you're demonstrating that he or she is more important to you at that moment than the person at the other end of the phone. This immediately makes you more likable. I'm sure that you, like me, have endured conversations in which the other person spent more time talking on the phone or texting than with you. I consider this rude, and have learned to stand up and tell the person we'll get together when he or she has time to talk. This usually encourages the person to put his or her phone away until our conversation is over.

Mirror the other person's posture, energy, and tone of voice. Mirroring the person's posture will occur automatically if you and the other person are interacting well.

Touching the other person for a brief moment increases your likability. Obviously, the touch needs to be nonthreatening and nonsexual. Because of this, the safest places to touch the other person are his or her shoulder, arm, or upper back.

These simple ideas can be used in any type of situation. You don't need to be the life and soul of the party to be liked. All you have to do is wear the appropriate clothes for the occasion, look happy, smile, make good eye contact, and be prepared to listen.

All of this might sound like a lot to learn. In practice, though, we make most of our decisions about other people in a matter of seconds. Scientists disagree about the specific amount of time involved, but agree that it takes a maximum of four minutes to make a permanent impression about someone we've just met.

The more elaborate our means of communication,
the less we communicate.
—JOSEPH PRIESTLEY

chapter six

FIRST IMPRESSIONS

Speed-dating has become a worldwide phenomenon. Eligible singles meet in groups and spend about three minutes talking one-on-one with each other. At the end of the evening, everyone marks a card saying which people they'd like to see again. The concept of speed-dating is based on the belief that you can learn enough about a person to evaluate his or her compatibility in just a few minutes.

There's an old adage that says, "You never get a second chance to make a good first impression." People start making their minds up about you the second they see you. By the time two minutes have passed, they have made a permanent assessment. Some people might take as long as four minutes, but this is still a very short period of time in which to make a potentially lifelong judgment. This two- to four-minute threshold applies in every type of situation, ranging from someone meeting a person of the opposite sex at a party, to a salesperson calling on a new client. By the time four minutes is up, you'll know how easy the other person will be to deal with, whether you like him or her, and if you want to continue getting to know the person better.

In the 1980s, Dr. Michael R. Solomon, a social psychologist and marketing expert, conducted research at the Graduate School of Business at New York University. His findings suggest people make eleven decisions about someone they've just met in the first seven seconds. These decisions are:

1. Economic level

2. Educational level and intelligence

3. Honesty and credibility

4. Trustworthiness

5. Level of sophistication

6. Gender, sexual orientation

7. Level of success

8. Political background

9. Values and principles

10. Ethnic background

11. Social desirability—would you like this person to be a friend?

After the vital first seven seconds, they spend the rest of the time they're together trying to confirm the accuracy of their assessment.[1]

Twenty years later, Janine Willis and Alexander Todorov at Princeton University conducted several experiments that show that we determine people's attractiveness, likability, honesty, competence, and aggressiveness after looking at their faces for a mere tenth of a second. The researchers also found that there was no significant difference between those instant decisions and those formed after looking at the person's face for a longer period of time.[2]

The first four minutes are vitally important in job interviews. Some people question this, as in a job interview the interviewer is doing most of the talking, and the applicant is using largely nonverbal gestures, such as eye contact, smiling, and nodding of the head. In actuality, what happens in those crucial first four minutes is more important than the applicant's qualifications and work experience, as the interviewer is determining if the person would fit in well with the people he or she would be working with. If the person is being interviewed for a sales role, the interviewer would want to make sure the person would get on well with their customers.

People are extremely reluctant to change their opinion of someone once they've made it. They even alter new information to make it fit the opinion they've already made. This may seem unfair, as none of us are at our best all the time. However, neglecting to make a good first impression can be expensive.

About thirty years ago, a new bread shop opened up close to our home. I was excited at the thought of being able to buy a variety of different breads within walking distance of our house. I could smell the aroma of freshly baked bread well before I reached the shop. When I went in, the bread was attractively displayed and I was keen to buy. There was no one behind the counter. I pressed the bell. I could hear someone out the back, but he or she did not respond. I pressed the bell again. Nothing happened. Finally, I called out, "Hello!"

A man in his middle thirties appeared, and with a snarl on his face, said, "Whaddaya want?" I stared at him for several seconds, turned around and walked home. I assumed he had been busy doing something out the back, and was annoyed at being interrupted. All the same, I never went inside his shop again, and wasn't surprised when the business closed down less than six months later.

This man had seen a wonderful business opportunity, but ruined it by failing to remember the "four-minute rule."

On another occasion, when I was a sales representative, I happened to visit a large printing company while the CEO was having a tantrum. One of his printers had ruined an expensive four-color printing job by getting the final color out of alignment. Because the mistake hadn't been picked up immediately, the printer had wasted more than $30,000 worth of highly expensive glossy paper. I had the misfortune to have an appointment with the CEO immediately after this had happened.

The appointment was a total waste of time, as he was highly stressed, angry, and wanted to lash out at someone. Once I realized this, I excused myself and made another appointment with his secretary for a few days later. When I returned, the man apologized and could not have been more charming, but I never felt comfortable with him after that, as I'd seen him at his worst in the vital first four minutes.

Because of this, you need to be aware of your body language when meeting people in every type of situation. As the conversation is likely to be small talk initially, nonverbal clues will help you decide whether or not you want to get to know the person. He or she will be observing your body language, too, for the same reason. To help make a good first impression, smile genuinely, listen to what the other person has to say, and see what you can learn from him or her. Be quick to thank anyone who treats you kindly. Be courteous, and treat the people you meet in the same way you like to be treated.

When people meet others in a social situation, they make plenty of eye contact, and usually smile. They may shake hands, nod and grin, wave, hug, do a high five, or anything else depending on the situation. After the initial introduction, the conversation will either continue or end after an exchange of pleasantries. If the meeting develops, the conversation will gradually go in other directions, and people will start to unconsciously mirror each other.

You subliminally notice people's nonverbal behavior when you first meet them, but it can be an interesting exercise to be consciously aware of someone's body language upon the first meeting. Here are some questions you might ask yourself: Does he look friendly? Does he make eye contact? Are his pupils dilated? Does he nod his head to encourage you to speak? Does he show interest by putting his head to one side? Are his gestures open or closed? What is his posture like? Do his words match his body language? Would you like to get to know him better?

A good friend of mine has the ability to get on with everyone. We often joke that if we wanted to complain about something, we'd ask him to do it for us, as he'd be able to resolve the problem and make a new friend at the same time. When I asked him about this talent, he told me that when he was a young man, his father had taught him to find something to like about everyone he met.

Although we assess others almost instantly, try not to judge them right away, as it's easy to make a mistake. If, for instance, someone looks anxious, worried, or unhappy when you first see them, this is the expression you'll judge them on. The person might normally be happy and jovial, but because you met them when they were concerned about something, your assessment will be wrong.

Be willing to modify your immediate evaluation of the people you meet as you learn more about them.

There is one important element of gaining rapport and being liked that we haven't discussed yet. That is the incredible power of touch, and we'll look at that in the next chapter.

Touch has a memory.

—JOHN KEATS

chapter seven

THE POWER OF TOUCH

As we rely so much on our eyes and ears, the sense of touch is often overlooked. It starts when a newborn baby is held for the first time, and the desire to be touched lasts throughout the person's life. The benefits of touch are incredible. Tiffany Field, Director of the Touch Research Institute at the University of Miami School of Medicine, has conducted a great deal of research on premature babies. In one experiment, a group of babies received fifteen-minute sessions of touch therapy every day for five to ten days. These babies gained 21 to 48 percent more weight than the premature babies who had received normal care and attention.[1]

A caring touch can instantly raise someone's spirits. Even an unintentional touch from a stranger can help people feel more positive. A touch can show support, express gratitude, convey sympathy, give encouragement, and add warmth to our personal communications. Because touching is so important to our wellbeing, I recommend therapeutic massages to people who do not receive regular touches from friends and family.

Haptics is the word used to describe any form of nonverbal communication that uses touch. Common examples are kissing, hugging, shaking hands, and touching someone on the shoulder.

An interesting experiment conducted in 2006 at DePauw University in Indiana demonstrated that people were able to identify a variety of emotions from a single touch by a stranger. The participants tried to convey twelve different emotions to volunteers who were not able to see them, or even see the touch being made on their forearms. Despite this, the results of this test varied from 48 percent to 83 percent, which is virtually the same as when the touching is done with both people able to see each other.[2]

It probably wasn't necessary to do the research, but it has been demonstrated that men respond more favorably to women who have lightly touched them on the arm.[3]

A gentle touch on the arm encouraged strangers to help someone pick up dropped belongings. In one experiment, people who were touched helped 90 percent of the time, while people who were not touched helped 63 percent of the time.[4]

Ongoing research by Professor Michael Lynn at the Cornell University School of Hotel Administration shows that lightly touching a customer on the shoulder or palm of the hand can increase the size of a tip dramatically. Customers who weren't touched left tips averaging 12 percent. Customers who were touched once on the shoulder left an average tip of 14 percent, and people who were touched twice on the hand left an average tip of 17 percent.[5]

The "prisoner's dilemma" is a game that gives players the opportunity to be either cooperative or selfish. Dr. Robert Kurzban, Associate Professor of Psychology at the University of Pennsylvania, conducted an interesting experiment that demonstrates the power of touch. Participants who were gently touched on the back as they started the game were much more likely to cooperate with the other participants than those who were not touched.

Because the power of touch has such a positive effect, it is an excellent and easy way to create rapport. A touch that lasts a mere fraction of a second can make the receiver of it feel happier, and he or she will also consider the person who gave the touch to be likable, caring, and kind.

In business situations, people usually touch someone to emphasize important aspects of what they're saying. This subliminally also adds credibility, as liars tend to avoid touching the people they're talking to. In the business world, the boss is usually the person who touches the subordinate. In today's corporate environment this needs to be done carefully to avoid misinterpretation, but a light touch on the shoulder or upper arm is usually accepted for what it is, especially if the boss is also saying, "Well done!"

The amount of touching varies from country to country around the world. Sidney Jourard (1926–1974), a Canadian psychologist, conducted a well-documented study in the 1960s on friends enjoying a conversation is cafes in different countries. Each conversation was observed for one hour. In the United Kingdom, the two friends did not touch each other at all. In the United States, the friends touched each other twice. In France, the touching was 110 times, and in Puerto Rico it increased to 180 times in an hour.[6]

There are some people whom you are not supposed to touch. You can, for instance, touch the Pope's hand, but cannot touch him anywhere else. In the United Kingdom, people feel strongly that the Queen should never be touched. Even when you're waiting in line to meet her, she has to offer her hand first for a handshake. This explains the protesting headlines in the British press when a Canadian provincial transport minister guided the Queen through a crowd by gently touching her elbow. In 1992, when Paul Keating, the then–prime minister of Australia, put his arm around the Queen, the *Evening Standard* ran a full-page article suggesting that all Australian expatriates be deported back to Australia.[7] In 2012, the Queen put her arm around Michelle Obama's waist in a friendly gesture, and Michelle responded by putting her arm around the Queen.[8] However, in this instance it was the Queen who made the first touch.

It's not only the Queen and the Pope who should not be touched. School teachers are taught not to casually touch their students. A friend of mine changed careers after he put his arm around a small girl to comfort her when he found her crying in the playground at his school. He was shocked that his instinctive desire to comfort and help was misconstrued, and gave up teaching as a result. Office workers are also taught to be careful about touching their fellow workers. Consequently, despite the value and importance of touch, it needs to be done appropriately and at the right time.

It's now time to make all of this information practical in the real world. As most people spend at least forty hours a week at work, we'll start, in the next chapter, by looking at how we can use our knowledge of body language in the workplace.

The time to stop talking is when the other person nods his head
affirmatively, but says nothing.
—HENRY S. HASKINS

chapter eight

SUCCESSFUL BODY LANGUAGE IN BUSINESS

Knowledge of body language gives you a huge advantage if you want to make a good impression in a job interview, progress in your career, get along well with your work colleagues, and enjoy the time you spend at work. Most people in the workforce spend at least forty hours a week at work, and for much of that time they're observed and judged by many people they interact with. It's important to get along well with your work colleagues, as you spend so much of your life with them. In actuality, your interactions with work colleagues are just as important as your ability to do your job.

Recently, I replaced my car. I don't enjoy doing this, as I find the process stressful. I know little about cars, and dislike the pushiness of many car salespeople. I was unlucky and met a stereotypical car salesman at the first place I went to. He was loud, condescending, and tried to sell me a car I had no interest in. He also totally ignored my wife, who was with me. He gave me a dominating handshake, and invited us into his office.

He leaned back in his chair, placed his hands behind his neck, and asked me what I was looking for. I could tell he wasn't interested as soon as I started talking. His eyes flicked all around the room, but seldom made any contact with mine. He interrupted me before I'd finished, telling me he had just the car for me. We went out to see it, and the car was virtually the complete opposite to what I wanted.

After that experience, it took me a few days to visit another car dealer. The salespeople I met after the first one were all courteous, pleasant, and tried to provide me with what I wanted. The man I eventually bought a car from made no attempt to sell it to me. He answered all my questions, offered to let me take the car home overnight if I wished, and suggested I take it to my mechanic to have him look at it. He was so laidback that it was hard to believe he sold cars.

From a body language point of view, he did everything right. He smiled when he greeted us, shook hands while making eye contact, and gave us his full attention while listening to what we had to say. He leaned forward, but did not enter our personal space. He made us feel relaxed. After buying the car, I sought out his boss to let him know how impressed we were with the salesman.

"He's our top salesman," he told us. "He's so quiet, you wouldn't know he's here, but he can certainly sell cars. I don't know how he does it."

The first salesman I spoke to probably makes a reasonable living. However, I'm sure the person I bought the car from makes much more money. They probably have the same amount of product knowledge, and spend similar amounts of time at work. Yet one of them is likely to be much more successful than the other.

No matter what work you do, your body language is being noticed by others. These people may not have studied the subject, but they'll instinctively make the assumption that someone who slouches and makes poor eye contact is lacking in confidence and people skills.

The Job Interview

Almost everyone finds job interviews stressful, and because of this many people do not sell themselves as well as they could. Fortunately, knowledge of body language can help you convey the right impression.

You should prepare for the interview ahead of time. Learn as much as you can about the company and the position you're applying for. Think about the questions you're likely to be asked, and answer them with as much detail as possible. If you do a search for "interview questions" on the Internet, you'll find plenty of questions to practice with. Along with the usual questions about where you worked before, and for how long, find answers for the more unusual questions you're likely to be asked. You might be asked: "What is your best quality?" "Why should we hire you?" "How would you describe yourself?" "What is your greatest weakness?"

An acquaintance of mine owns a food manufacturing company, and its products are exported to several different countries. He complained to me that most people who applied for positions in his company had no idea what the company manufactured and were surprised to learn that they exported almost half of their production.

"I want people who are passionate about my company," he told me. "How can they be passionate when they don't even know what we produce?"

You should also think of the impression you want to project in the interview. Ideally, if you want the position, you should be interested in the company, feel convinced that you can do the job well, and be keen to be part of the organization. You can convey all of this with your body language.

Dress appropriately for the position you're applying for. You don't need to wear a suit if you're applying for a manual labor position. Neither should you dress casually if applying for an entry-level position in the corporate world. It's important to think carefully about what you'll wear, as this will be one of the first things the interviewer will see when you walk into his or her office.

People who are clothes conscious are perceived, rightly or wrongly, as having higher self-esteem and will perform better in the job. The clothes you choose should be reasonably conservative, and convey the impression that you're capable and reliable. Make sure your shoes are clean, your nails are well-groomed, and your hair is clean and tidy. Remember that people with short hair are perceived as being more competent than people with long hair. This applies to both men and women. Consequently, it's a good idea to have your hair cut if necessary.

Dr. Judith A. Waters, a psychology professor at Fairleigh Dickinson University in Teaneck, New Jersey, conducted an experiment to test the results of good grooming. She sent out identical résumés to more than three hundred companies. These contained either "before" or "after" photographs of the applicants. The "before" photographs showed the applicant dressed casually and looking unkempt. The "after" photographs showed the same person appearing well-dressed and well-groomed. No company received both "before" and "after" photographs of the same applicant. Dr. Waters asked the companies to give an approximate starting salary for each applicant. In every case, the salaries were 8 to 20 percent higher for the people whose résumés contained the "after" photograph.[1]

No matter how you feel inside, project confidence when you arrive at the interview. Be aware that you might be observed from the moment you arrive at the company. Look happy. You may well be nervous, but you mustn't show it. Crossed arms or feet, coupled with fidgeting, a lack of smiles and poor eye contact, tell the interviewer that you're stressed and nervous.

You should have a firm handshake, but make it no firmer than the shake of the interviewer. This is especially the case if you're a man being interviewed by a woman. Your palm should be offered in a vertical position. The interviewer will probably offer his or her hand first, but be prepared to offer yours if necessary. Smile and make eye contact as you shake hands. Your smile should be a genuine one, with your teeth visible. If your smile is genuine, you'll give an eyebrow flash automatically.

If you're offered a choice of seats, choose a chair beside the interviewer's desk, rather than across from it. In many cases, the interviewer will not sit behind his or her desk anyway, as it creates a barrier. If you have to sit down directly across from the interviewer, turn your chair as you sit down, so your body is not directly facing the interviewer. Once you've sat down, keep your body straight, and lean forward slightly to show interest. This makes you look keen and enthusiastic. Make good eye contact during the interview, but don't stare at the interviewer.

You should place both feet flat on the floor, or, if you prefer, cross them at the ankles. Keep your feet still, if possible, and avoid jiggling a foot, as this gives the impression of boredom and uneasiness.

Be aware of your body language. One of the most common mistakes is to smile at inappropriate times. This makes you appear weak, unassertive, and nervous. The interviewer will expect you to be nervous, but you don't want to make this obvious.

Make good eye contact. This makes you appear confident, dependable, responsible, and honest. Listen carefully and look interested in what the interviewer is saying. You might angle your head slightly, and nod every now and again. Look happy, and smile when it's appropriate.

Keep your hands away from your face. Relax as much as you can, and avoid crossing your arms and legs. Open body language makes you appear interested and confident.

When people are nervous, they often don't know what to do with their hands. Do not cross your arms, as that creates a barrier and makes you appear defensive. It's much better to rest your hands in your lap, raising them to make gestures when necessary. As much as possible, avoid touching your face. This is a sign of nervousness, but can indicate dishonesty. You don't want the interviewer to make either of these assessments.

When I was a teenager, my father gave me a good tip about controlling nervousness. He told me that while I was worrying about how I appeared to the other person, the other person was probably experiencing the exact same feelings. Consequently, to eliminate my nervousness, all I had to do was make the other person feel comfortable. I quickly discovered that when I did that, my nervousness completely disappeared, as I was no longer concerned about my perceived inadequacies.

Pay attention to the body language of the interviewer. Initially, he or she will try to establish rapport, as people are more likely to be honest when they feel relaxed and comfortable. The interviewer will know that you're likely to be nervous, especially if you really want the position.

A common technique is for the interviewer to offer the candidate tea or coffee. As nervous people are likely to decline the offer, the interviewer is likely to say that he or she is getting a drink, and could he or she get you one at the same time? Obviously, you can't cross your arms while holding a cup. Consequently, handing you a drink forces you to adopt a more open posture, and become less defensive.

As you become more confident during the interview, you might start mirroring some of the interviewer's body language. However, be extremely careful with this, as you don't want the interviewer to become aware that you're doing it.

The person who is interviewing you will have a variety of ways to encourage you to talk. Ideally, he or she will want you to talk about three times as much as he or she does. To do this, he or she will use a variety of techniques, including head-nodding and gesturing with the hands. A slow nod encourages you to continue talking, while more rapid nodding signifies agreement. The interviewer will also modify his or her posture and facial expressions to encourage you to talk. Naturally, the interviewer will also speak, and will change his or her tone of voice from time to time, to encourage you to reveal as much of yourself as possible.

However, I've known interviewers who deliberately frown, make little eye contact, and appear bored, just to see how the applicant reacts. Consequently, you can't assume that the interviewer's body language represents their true feelings. In many cases, the interviewer doesn't have the authority to employ you. He or she conducts interviews, and passes the findings on to someone else who makes the final decision. You need to remain professional, no matter what body language the interviewer projects.

There are nonverbal indications that the interview has gone well. It's a positive sign if the interviewer gives you his or her full attention and smiles frequently. The interviewer is genuinely interested in you if he or she nods frequently, and leans toward you during the interview.

At the end of the interview, shake hands again, smile, and thank the interviewer for seeing you.

Climbing the Ladder

Once you have the position, you need to start thinking about the future. If you have no ambition, you can focus on the job at hand, and live from day to day. However, if you want to get promoted, you need to be exceptional in your current position, and you also need to display successful body language.

This starts every morning when you arrive at work. Just before you walk in, loosen your shoulders, put a smile on your face, and say a cheerful "Good morning" to everyone you see. The feelings of positivity and energy you get from this will last throughout the day, and other people will view you as someone who is energetic, enthusiastic, and friendly.

When meeting new people, greet them with enthusiasm. Let your genuine smile, open body language, and friendly words tell them what a wonderful person you are. Enthusiasm and energy are two of the most positive qualities you can have in the workplace. They mean you'll be noticed, and will attract favorable comments. When an opportunity for promotion becomes available, you'll be seriously considered for the opportunity.

Over the years, many people have complained to me that they seemed to be stuck in their present position, while people with less ability were promoted. As I'm usually hearing this from the point of view of the people who are stalled in their careers, it's impossible to know if the people who are getting promoted have greater or lesser ability. However, I know the chances are that the people who get promoted are consciously or unconsciously making better use of body language.

If you want to progress in your career, look happy. Smile. Look people in the eye. Develop a good handshake. Pay attention to your posture, both standing and sitting. Be positive, cheerful, and enthusiastic. Be approachable. Listen, and be willing to help others. Keep up-to-date on what is going on in your field, and be willing to share this information with others. Use mirroring to create rapport with people who are at the same level as you, or lower. Avoid mirroring people who are higher up the promotion ladder than you, as it might be perceived as pride and overconfidence. In addition, resist the urge to repeat any gossip you may hear.

You can be doing all of that automatically in twenty-eight days, as that's how long it takes to change a habit. You can test this by moving your wastepaper basket from one side of your desk to the other. For approximately four weeks you'll go to toss the trash in the direction the waste paper basket used to be, but after that time you'll toss it in the right direction without even thinking about it.

You should evaluate yourself for any negative body language you may be expressing. You might slouch, for instance, or make poor eye contact. You might frown constantly. You may have some nervous mannerisms, such as jingling coins in your pocket, or jiggling a foot. You might have a limp handshake. These are all simple things to rectify, and they can make a great difference in how you're perceived by others.

One woman I knew was fired from the company she worked for. Later, she was told that everyone had got tired of her constant sighs. People avoided her, as no matter what they said, she'd respond with a sigh. It was simply a habit that had gotten out of control, but it was an expensive one that cost her a job that she loved.

When I started my career in publishing, one of the other trainees was called "the creep" behind his back. This was because he stared into people's eyes, and never appeared to blink. The fact that he never looked away unnerved everyone in the office. I have no idea if he thought he was making good eye contact, or was deliberately using his eyes to dominate others. He was intelligent and ambitious, but lasted only a matter of months before abandoning his publishing career.

By working hard and displaying good body language, you'll tell everyone that you're capable, conscientious, enthusiastic, and professional. You'll also be highly promotable.

Body Language in Sales

You need to sell yourself before you start selling your product. This means gaining rapport with your prospects before you can sell to them. The amount of time this takes differs from person to person. Trust is gained gradually, but it can be lost quickly. If you try to make a sale before the prospect feels he or she trusts you, you'll be seen as aggressive and pushy.

When meeting potential clients, you should give them a reasonably firm handshake while smiling and looking them in the eye.

You need to be aware of the spatial bubbles we all live within. You'll put the prospect off if you stand too close to him or her, especially in the early stages of the sales process. You should remain in the business zone, which is approximately four feet apart, until you've become trusted by the prospect. As people enjoy buying from people who are physically close to them, you might bridge this gap by handing the prospect something to look at or read. If the prospect steps back or crosses his or her arms defensively, you'll know that you've moved too close, too quickly, and should slow the whole process down until the prospect becomes more relaxed.

A genuine smile tells the prospect that you're friendly, approachable, and open. Don't overdo the size of the smile. If you walk into the room with a broad smile on your face, your prospect is likely to feel confused and wonder what your motivations are.

People's hands are more likely to be visible when they're being honest and sincere. When someone is exaggerating, or telling a lie, his or her hand movements will be fewer, and the hands may be placed in the person's pockets, or hidden behind a desk. Consequently, use your hands naturally, and let them be seen.

Mirror the prospect's body language, but be careful not to make it obvious. If the prospect has crossed his or her arms, you might do the same, even though this is considered a barrier. After a while, uncross your arms. If you're in rapport, the prospect will do the same. If the prospect's arms remain crossed, cross your arms again, and try uncrossing them again later.

Make good eye contact with the prospect, but don't hold the gaze for too long—this can be considered aggressive. However, you also don't want to avoid eye contact, as this makes you appear dishonest, or lacking in confidence.

When you sit down to discuss the proposed sale, try to sit at a forty-five-degree angle to your prospect. This is less confrontational than sitting directly opposite him or her. If you've taken the prospect out of his or her office to discuss the proposal, allow the prospect to sit with his or her back to a wall, as this provides symbolic protection, and helps him or her feel more at ease.

Sometimes, you'll be selling to a group of people. You must watch the body language of all of them, and ensure that you retain the attention of everyone. Even if you know the decision maker, make your proposal to everyone.

I learned this the hard way more than thirty years ago, when I was selling printing machinery. My boss and I arrived for our appointment with a large printing company. My boss knew the CEO, and they had a brief chat before the meeting began. At the meeting, the CEO sat at one end of a long boardroom table, and several of his executives sat along one side. My boss and I were placed in the middle of the other side. It was a rather awkward arrangement from our point of view, and was probably done deliberately to make us feel uncomfortable. My boss did almost all of the talking. I was there largely to provide the factual information about the machine we were trying to sell.

My boss totally ignored the executives facing him, and directed his sales pitch at the CEO. It was interesting to watch the executives become more and more closed as the meeting progressed. At the start of the meeting, they leaned forward and looked interested. However, they gradually moved back from the table, and crossed their arms. One appeared to be taking notes, but as we got up to leave I discovered he'd drawn an elaborate doodle on his pad.

There were no questions when my boss finished his sales pitch. The CEO said he'd discuss the proposal with his executives, and get back to us.

In the car going back to the office, my boss was ecstatic, as he was convinced the sale was assured. I wasn't nearly as confident, but kept my thoughts to myself. A few days later, my boss phoned the CEO and was told the board was still considering the proposal. A few days after that, I was sent to visit them to see if I could get the signed contract.

I spoke with the executive I normally met with on my visits to this corporation. He told me they'd signed an agreement with a different company for a machine that was markedly inferior to the one we were offering. When I asked why they'd done this, he told me that the executives had felt snubbed and excluded from the negotiation, and had all voted in favor of the opposition's printing press.

My boss was furious when he heard the news, and blamed everyone except himself. However, he learned from the experience, and included everyone in group sales meetings from that time on.

There's another reason why you should include everyone present in the sales process. Frequently, the decision maker wants to listen to the questions raised by the other members of his or her team, and keeps a deliberately inactive role, as this gives him or her time to think.

Body Language in Management

You've worked hard, paid your dues, and finally you've attained the position you've always dreamed about. You're now in a leadership role, and you need to portray that in everything you do and say.

Naturally, you need to appear confident and in control. You do this by walking tall, making good eye contact, developing a good handshake, smiling, and being a good listener. You've learned all of these as you've progressed in your career. However, you now need more than this.

Experiments at Harvard and Columbia Business Schools show that holding your body in a powerful pose for two minutes increases your levels of testosterone, which is linked to confidence and power, and lowers your levels of cortisol, a major stress hormone. There are three main power poses. You can stand with your arms and legs stretched out, you can lean over your desk with your arms placed wide apart, or you can lean back with your hands linked behind your head and your feet resting on your desk.[2] You should do this privately, before any situation in which you want to feel more confident.

You need to become a good listener. Face the person you are speaking with, and make good eye contact. This shows interest. Stand up straight, or lean forward if you're sitting. Nod your head, use facial expressions to convey your feelings, and make other indications that you're listening carefully. It's important that other people know you're giving them your full attention, and that you're interested and care. Consequently, ignore any interruptions or distractions, such as text messages, emails, phone calls, or papers on your desk. Don't look at your watch, as this can indicate that you feel the other person is preventing you from doing something more important.

Remove any barriers between you and the person you're speaking with. You might move from behind your desk. Avoid crossing your arms, as this can be viewed as a barrier, or a sign of disagreement.

One interesting barrier occurs when someone sits down straddling a chair with the back of it providing symbolic protection. Although this person is using the back of the chair for protection, he or she wants to control and dominate the group. The protection is needed in order to repel anyone resenting this person's confrontational attitude.

Develop a strong, genuine handshake. You don't want to give anyone a bone cruncher, or an overly limp handshake. Avoid giving a dominant handshake. Give a genuine smile and make eye contact as you shake hands. Practice your handshake with someone you trust, until you develop one you're happy with. If you have a senior role in a corporation, you'll be shaking hands with people regularly, and will be judged by it.

Be generous with your smiles. Most people smile back when they receive a smile. Smiling makes you feel good, and raises the spirits of everyone around you. It also makes you appear more approachable.

Use your hands. It's been demonstrated that gesturing improves the quality of speech, as it activates part of the brain known as the Broca's area, which stimulates thoughts and speech.[3] However, don't move your hands mindlessly. Use them to emphasize points, and to act as punctuation to what you're saying. Be careful with gestures when in foreign countries, or when dealing with people from other cultures.

Recently, I saw a TV interview with Brendan Marrocco, a young soldier who lost all four limbs when he was wounded by a bomb in Iraq in 2009. Skilled surgeons were able to give him two replacement arms. In the interview, he made the point that it's hard to have a conversation without using your hands and arms. "Not having arms takes so much away from you. Even your personality, you know. You talk with your hands. You do everything with your hands, and when you don't have that, you're kind of lost for a while," he said.[4]

Remain calm, even in stressful situations. This enables you to stay in charge, no matter what is going on. You can't control or lead when you're agitated, nervous, or stressed. If you become upset, your subordinates will also become emotional and make the situation worse. When you're stressed, you'll find it hard to read other people's body language, and will send off confusing nonverbal signals. Stress upsets your body chemistry, and affects people in different ways. Headaches, upset stomachs, palpitations, rapid breathing, panic attacks, trembling, and a dry mouth are some of the most commonly seen symptoms of major stress.

Do not raise your voice when speaking to subordinates, no matter how angry you are. Many years ago, I had a boss who yelled and screamed at the slightest provocation, and couldn't understand why no one worked with him for long. Remain aware of your emotions.

If possible, take a few minutes out to calm yourself down. Take slow, deep breaths until you feel calm enough to handle the situation. One useful technique is to take in long, deep breaths, hold them for a couple of seconds, and exhale with a sigh. Stress gathers around the shoulders, so rolling your shoulders while breathing slowly can also help.

Even if you find it hard to relax completely, remember that if you appear to be calm, you'll be able to persuade others.

You'll probably need to give speeches from time to time, and may need to learn how to express yourself verbally and nonverbally in front of an audience. The most important part is to make sure that your words and body language are congruent. If you send out nonverbal signals that match what you're saying, your audience will subliminally pick up on this and believe what you're saying. You also want to make sure that your voice conveys warmth, confidence, and sincerity.

A few months ago, I heard a speaker tell his audience that he'd be delighted to answer any questions. As he said this, his hands made brushing movements that pushed the audience away. Needless to say, no one had a question for him.

When chairing meetings, you'll be able to use your body language skills to observe the people attending. This enables you to be aware of their body language and determine their views, attitudes, and feelings. You'll notice their inconsistencies when what they say doesn't match their body language. You'll also notice when their words and body language match. Observing the other people also forces them to remain active and involved, as they know they're being watched.

Trust your intuition. Dr. Jonas Salk (1914–1995), the inventor of the polio vaccine, said, "The intuitive mind tells the logical mind where to look next." There are many examples of business executives making successful decisions based on their intuition. When something feels right, it usually is. If it feels wrong, your intuition is warning you to stay away. You may not consciously notice when someone's body language is not congruent with what he or she is saying, but you may pick this up intuitively. Coupling your intuition with body language enables you to notice things that are invisible to everyone else.

You have also earned the right to demonstrate your power in subtle ways. You can lean back in your chair and clasp your hands behind your head. You can steeple your hands. You can own more space by spreading out in your chair and placing an arm over the back of an adjacent chair. However, you must also remain aware that there's a time and a place for these gestures.

Office Parties

Office parties are a good way for members of the staff to relax and get to know each other better. However, it can be a potential minefield, and virtually everyone knows stories about people who made fools of themselves by drinking too much and acting inappropriately at an office function.

Getting along with work colleagues is vitally important in a successful career. People who are approachable, friendly, and easy to get along with are more likely to be promoted than their unfriendly, unhelpful colleagues.

Office parties provide a good opportunity to network, meet staff members from different departments, and impress others with your sociability and communication skills. If you do all of this, office parties are an effective way to get noticed by people who can help you progress in your career.

The most important thing to remember is that an office party is an excuse to network. Consequently, you need to be careful with alcohol. You don't need to get drunk to have a good time. You can ruin the evening, and even your entire career, by overindulging at a work party. If you drink too much, you're likely to say and do things that you'd never dream of doing or saying sober.

Smile and look happy before you enter the room where the party is being held. Greet people in whatever manner is appropriate in the company you work in. You might exchange handshakes, daps, hugs, or high fives, and possibly a mixture of these. If you're shaking hands, make sure that you offer your hand vertically, with the thumb on top and the little finger underneath. Office parties are not a good place to try out the dominant handshake, and you don't want to use a submissive handshake either.

Exhibit an open posture. Avoid crossing your arms or even holding your glass with both hands, as this also creates a psychological barrier. Stand evenly on both feet, and look as if you're enjoying yourself, even if you're not. If you stand with an open posture, other people will feel relaxed around you. If you stand with your arms, and possibly legs, crossed you'll appear defensive and unapproachable.

Smile and laugh whenever it's appropriate. Everyone knows they should always laugh at the boss's jokes. Laughter is contagious, and increases the connection between members of a group.

Posture

Few people pay attention to their posture. They'd be amazed to learn that a few small changes in the way they stand, sit, and walk can transform the way in which others viewed them. Slouching is a good example. Someone who is slouching is hunched over, and usually looks downward. People who slouch appear weak, timid, listless, insecure, unapproachable, and lacking in confidence. It's sometimes a sign of boredom or depression. It's also potentially damaging to the person's health, as slouching can cause headaches and backache.

None of this portrays confidence to others. A boss would be likely to overlook a staff member who is slouching, and ask someone who appeared more energetic to take on an important task. Would you approach someone who is slouching and ask him or her for a date?

Fortunately, it's easy to remedy a slouch. All the person need do is raise his or her head, and pull the shoulders back. This will immediately change the person's appearance, and make him or her more appealing to others. In addition, he or she will feel more powerful and confident, and will feel better about him- or herself. As a bonus, he or she will become slightly taller, as standing up straight increases the person's height. Do you remember your mother telling you to stand up straight? It was good advice, as your mother knew that height is associated with power, influence, and confidence.

You can test the difference standing up straight makes to your appearance easily for yourself. Stand in front of a full-length mirror, and examine yourself. Notice how you're standing, where your arms are, the position of your head, and the expression you're wearing. What message does all of this convey to you?

Once you've done that, walk away and decide how you want to be perceived by others. This will automatically change your posture. Return to the mirror and notice any changes in your posture. You can also experiment by pretending to be miserable, bored, angry, confident, and submissive. You'll find that even pretending to have these feelings changes your posture. If you maintain the posture, you'll stop pretending, and will start to experience the feelings.

While you're checking yourself out in the mirror, look at your facial expression when it's in repose. You may find that your mouth turns down at the corners, or you might appear to squint or frown. People will assume that your facial expression reveals your character.

If you see that your facial expression indicates sadness, grumpiness, worry, or anything else, start doing something about it. If you want to come across as someone who's open and friendly, try smiling more often. Practice your smile in front of the mirror. It takes time to change your habitual facial expression, but it's worth doing if you want people to see you as a happy and friendly person.

Now that you know how your feelings influence your posture, decide on the image you wish to present to the world, and focus on that every time you're out and about. Within a matter of weeks, you'll no longer have to consciously think about it, as it will become a natural part of your life. When you achieve this, you'll be projecting your desired image all the time.

Your posture can also be detected by people speaking to you on the phone. This is because your posture affects your breathing, and even causes slight changes in your voice. Make sure you stand up or sit up straight when talking on the phone. You'll sound positive and enthusiastic if you smile when you answer the phone. If you're middle-aged or older, doing this will make you sound younger, too. Standing up has another benefit, too. It makes you feel more confident, and you'll be able to make decisions more easily. I'm often asked if people should make their usual hand gestures when talking on the phone. Obviously, these can't be seen by the person you're speaking to, but they'll add power and forcefulness to your voice.

The clothes you wear also tell people about you. You'll naturally feel more confident when you're well dressed. Obviously, what you wear is determined by your position in the company, and the particular job you do. The janitor doesn't need to wear a suit, but sales staff and management might. You might be limited in what you can reasonably wear at work. Many people wear a uniform, for instance. Even if you don't wear a uniform, the type of work you do and company policies will influence what you can and can't wear. Even the particular tasks you do on different days could influence what you wear. One of my sons works in advertising. He wears smart, but casual, clothes to work most of the time.

However, he also keeps a suit and tie in his office that he changes into if he needs to see a client. Once the business meeting is over, he'll put on his casual clothes again.

If you choose to go against the dress code of your company or occupation, you might be viewed negatively and this would affect your chances of promotion.

Not long ago, I had to visit my attorney. Each time I see him, he's wearing a dark suit, with a white shirt and blue tie. His shoes gleam with polish. If I arrived one day and found him wearing dirty jeans and a T-shirt, I'd be flabbergasted. I want my lawyer to be conservatively dressed. I know the clothes he wears make no difference on how good he is at his job, but I'm sure he'd lose a lot of business if he started wearing casual clothes to work. This is because people expect middle-aged attorneys to wear good-quality suits. Dress codes are becoming more casual, but we still make judgments about what people wear.

In business, if you want to convey an image of authority and success, you should dress more formally than the staff who are subordinate to you. People tend to think that dark suits are associated with honesty and a serious approach, while lighter colors are associated with casual occasions. Certainly, slightly conservative clothes are a safer bet than something that's ostentatious or totally inappropriate.

No matter what position you hold in the company, you should dress with propriety. You should also ensure your shoes are polished, your hair and nails are clean, and your clothes are clean and smart.

If you combine appropriate clothing with good posture, you have a winning combination that will help you progress in your career.

There's an old saying that you should dress for the job you're aiming for. This is good in theory, but may not be practical. It might cause conflict with your fellow workers, especially if it made you stand out from the crowd. If you're a plumber who is aiming for a management role, you won't want to wear a suit and tie as long as you're performing a hands-on job.

As well as your clothes, you might like to consider what you surround yourself with in your workplace, as these will all be noted and evaluated by others. Even your choice of cell phone affects the impression you make on others.

Have you ever considered the words "your Highness" and "He's a low-life?" What about "He's on his high horse," and someone who is "looked down on"? These all relate to status.

No matter how tall or short you might be, you don't want your height to affect the interaction. One way of adjusting a discrepancy in height is to stand back a little bit so you're not looking directly up or down on the other person.

There are times when you might want to appear smaller than you are. You might do this, for instance, if you're dealing with a client who is shorter than you. In this situation, you don't want to appear to be dominating the situation. You can do this by suggesting you both sit down. Alternatively, you might take a step back, or stoop slightly.

If you have a desk job, sit straight, and keep your back parallel to the back of the chair. This makes you look confident and capable. Sitting with a straight back, with your feet flat on the floor and facing forward, conveys confidence and self-assurance.

Body postures can be classified into two groups: closed and open. If someone is sitting with her arms folded, legs crossed, and her entire body turned away, she's exhibiting a closed posture. If she's sitting with her arms and legs uncrossed, and her palms visible, she's showing an open posture. An open posture is a sign of openness, friendliness, and a willingness to connect with others. People with an open posture are better liked, and are easier to deal with than people with a closed posture. It's also much easier to persuade or influence others using an open posture. President Barack Obama is a good example of someone who uses an open posture to good effect. He also stands up straight, and this makes him look energetic and enthusiastic.

A highly effective way to get on with others is to lean forward toward the other person, especially when you are both sitting down. Someone who leans back is subconsciously distancing him- or herself. It can also indicate dislike, or be done deliberately in an attempt to control and dominate. Someone who leans in is showing that he or she likes the other person, and is interested in hearing what they have to say. However, you need to be cautious with this when you meet someone for the first time, as the other person might think you're encroaching on his or her personal space if you lean too far forward.

Mirroring, or imitating, the posture of the person you're dealing with makes the interaction more pleasant, as it gives the impression that you both have the same goals. Most of the time, the subordinate person mirrors the posture of the person who is senior, rather than the other way around. Mirroring is something that's done subconsciously when we're in harmony with someone else. The technical term for this is *limbic synchrony*. If you're enjoying a chat with a close friend, you'll find that you'll sit in the same way, and your arms and legs will mirror each other.

Mirroring can also be done deliberately to gain rapport. Salespeople are taught how to do this, as it's much easier to sell something when the salesperson and the potential buyer are in rapport.

Another advantage of mirroring someone's body language is that it enables you to gain an idea of what the other person is experiencing, and see what is going on from his or her point of view. This is because our bodies and emotions are closely connected.

Men are often reluctant to mirror a woman's posture. However, they can gain rapport by mirroring her facial expressions while listening. Women tend to display more facial expressions than men, as many men deliberately try to appear as unemotional as possible.

Whenever you feel sad or unhappy for any reason, change your posture and notice how much better you feel. Changing your posture changes your mood, and immediately makes you feel more positive and alive.

You can make good use of all these skills if you're trying to find a romantic partner. However, there are many other signals that can be learned to help you nonverbally tell someone you're interested in him or her. You also need to be able to recognize the signals that are being sent to you. That is the topic of the next chapter.

Came but for friendship, and took away love.
—THOMAS MOORE

chapter nine

THE BODY LANGUAGE OF LOVE AND ROMANCE

When I was twenty years old, I worked for my passage from New Zealand to the United Kingdom as a steward on a ship. I shared a cabin with five other young men, and we spent most of our spare time talking about women and the different techniques we used to try to meet them. Fortunately for me, they had all made several previous trips on this ship, and knew where to find parties at every port. It became apparent at the first port that one of the men was a master at picking up women. We were invited to a party, and less than ten minutes after we arrived, he left with an attractive young lady. When we got back to the ship, I asked him if he had met her on previous visits. "No," he replied. "I'd never seen her before." The rest of us had had no success whatsoever. My other cabin mates called him "Lucky," as he managed to do this at every port of call.

Sure enough, he did the same thing at the next port, though this time it must have taken him thirty minutes to leave the party with a girl. When we reached Panama, I was determined to discover the secret of his success. I watched him closely, and was mystified as he quietly surveyed the room until he found a lady he wished to talk to. He introduced himself, chatted with her for a while, and then left the party with her. I watched him do this again in Fort Lauderdale, Florida; Kingston, Jamaica; and Bermuda. I left the ship in London none the wiser. It puzzled me for a long time. He was of average height and had an unremarkable face and physique. He wasn't the sort of person anyone would look at twice. However, he knew something that I didn't.

It took me years to realize that this young man knew how to send out, and receive, the right body language signals. I don't know if he'd learned them somewhere, or if it was instinctive. He certainly wasn't prepared to discuss them with his cabin mates.

I constantly meet people who experience problems in flirting, dating, and often simply meeting potential partners. In most cases, the problems arise because the person either doesn't see, or alternatively misunderstands, the nonverbal messages being sent to them. Women are usually better at reading these signals than men. Most of the time, women have to make the first move, too, and are often frustrated when the subtle signals they send out are not recognized.

I saw a striking example of this a few months ago at an engagement party. Most of the guests were in their twenties, and it was fascinating to watch their body language as they interacted with each other.

One of the guests was a seemingly shy young man who didn't appear to know anyone. He stood with his arms clasped in front of him. His shoulders were slumped, and he had a trace of a nervous smile on his face. He separated his hands only when he took a sip from his drink that was sitting on a table beside him.

Several feet away were four young women who obviously knew each other well. They were happy, relaxed, and enjoying the evening. I noticed that one of these women kept glancing at the young man. Each time they made eye contact, she smiled and looked away. This is a sign that the woman is approachable. She touched her neck, and changed her position slightly so she was facing him directly. The young man appeared oblivious to all of these signs of interest.

The woman continued her conversation with her friends, but kept glancing at the man who appeared to be more interested in his drink than in meeting an attractive young woman. She ran her fingers through her hair, idly stroked her neck and throat, and tilted her head. He still seemed unaware of what she was doing.

Finally, she excused herself from the group and went over to speak to the young man. His face flushed, and I could see his Adam's apple bobbing up and down. For the first couple of minutes, she did most of the talking, but gradually it became a conversation—when the evening ended they were still together and he was holding her hand.

There could have been a number of reasons why this man failed to recognize any of the signals she was sending him. He seemed to know no one at the party so he may have been feeling sorry for himself and oblivious to what was going on around him. He may have seen the signals, but wasn't brave enough to approach her. The most likely explanation is that, being male, he simply failed to recognize them.

A few days ago, while waiting in line for movie tickets, I happened to overhear part of a conversation between two young men.

"Jean's really keen on you!" one of them said.

"Really?" replied the other, obviously surprised.

"Yes. You must have seen the way she looks at you."

"Can't say I have. What do you mean?"

"Oh, the way she looks at you all the time with a smile on her face. Her eyes go soft, and she licks her lips, and she strokes her neck. Surely you've noticed."

"Can't say I have."

If you're searching for a partner, the information in this chapter will help you recognize the courtship signals aimed at you, and will also enable you to send out appropriate courtship signals to others.

Female Courtship Signals

Eyes

Brief eye contact, followed by a slight smile, is usually the first step in telling a man that she's interested in him. This is often done with a sideways glance. The first time she does this, the eye contact is for only a second or two. If the man is interested, he'll keep watching the woman to see if she looks at him again. Usually, she'll have to repeat it three times before the man realizes what she's doing. If the man fails to recognize these signals, the woman can wait a minute or two, and then give him a longer glance, accompanied by a wider smile. If the man fails to approach after this, it's up to the woman to decide whether or not to approach him. This is better than sending him small smiles all night.

The pupils dilate to express interest. This is entirely involuntary. Some women deliberately widen their eyes when talking to a prospective partner. This gesture makes them appear young and helpless, which is usually not the case. However, if the eyes are widened too much, the person looks scared, rather than flirtatious. Frequently, an increase in the amount of blinking reveals the person's interest.

Smiles

A slight, momentary smile that is repeated a few times indicates interest. After each smile, the woman looks away. A minute later, she looks back, smiles again, and looks away. She may have to do this a number of times before the man realizes what she's doing. Sometimes the head is tilted and one shoulder is slightly raised to create an impression of submissiveness.

Research has shown that men don't usually approach a woman until she's given him a nonverbal indication of her interest. A smile, accompanied by an eyebrow flash, is the most usual way of doing this.[1]

Once the man and woman have become acquainted, a genuine smile while speaking is the best way for the woman to let him know she finds him attractive.

Hair

Women sometimes play with their hair. They may pat, twirl, or smooth their hair, run their fingers through it, or toss their head to flick their hair back and expose their face.

Neck

The neck is a vulnerable area, and women frequently touch it as part of a flirting ritual. They may also touch other parts of their body.

Lips

Women often lick their lips to encourage the person to think about what kissing them would be like. This gesture is provocative, and the man will think she is leading him on. If you're not ready to go to bed with him, you should use this gesture with care.

Knee and Foot

If the woman is sitting down, she may point her knee or foot toward the person she is attracted to. If she's standing up, her foot will be angled toward the person.

Legs

If the woman is sitting down, she might intertwine her legs to draw attention to them, and to make them appear more attractive. Crossing and uncrossing her legs serves the same function. She may stroke her thighs while doing this.

She is also likely to open her legs slightly. She can do this whether sitting or standing. This is contrary to the advice her mother probably gave her about keeping her legs together, or crossed, at all times.

She may sit with one leg crossed over the other. Her knee will point toward the person she's interested in. This position provides the other person with a tantalizing glimpse of her thighs.

Clothes

Women sometimes smooth their clothes as a preening gesture. This is normally accompanied by touching various parts of the body, such as the thighs, neck, and face.

Palms and Wrists

Once the two people are talking, the woman will expose her palms and wrist. The vulnerable wrists are considered a powerful erogenous zone.

Touch

After the couple have chatted for a while, the woman will touch the man lightly on the arm. This can be done deliberately or apparently accidentally. She will watch to see how the man reacts to this, before touching him again. Touching takes the meeting to a different level of intimacy.

Male Courtship Signals

Posture

Men correct their posture by standing more erect, pulling their stomachs in, and raising their heads slightly. This is largely unconscious. Once they've made contact, the man might stand with his thumbs in his belt and his fingers pointing toward his genitals.

Eyes

When a man sees a woman he likes, he'll do an involuntary eyebrow flash to express his interest.

Men will increase their gaze and allow their eyes to move around the woman's face from eye level to the chin. The eyes will dilate involuntarily to reveal their interest.

Once the man and woman have started talking, the man can increase his chances dramatically by focusing his full attention on her. When he isn't making direct eye contact, he should let his eyes explore her face. Men with "wandering eyes" are not considered anywhere near as attractive as men who use their eyes appropriately.

Self-grooming

Men become aware of their appearance and start grooming themselves. They might smooth their hair, straighten their tie, brush invisible specks off their clothing, and touch their collar and cuffs. This preening behavior can be found throughout the animal kingdom.

Courtship Tips

If you're hoping to meet someone, be brave enough to move away from the group of friends you happen to be with. Someone who'd love to meet you might find the prospect of interacting with a group of strangers too intimidating.

Keep your posture open. Make sure your arms and legs are uncrossed. If someone's arms remain crossed after you've met him or her, it's probably a sign that the person isn't interested. Keep your hands out of your pockets. Hands in pockets sends a message that you don't want to engage in conversation.

If the person you've just met keeps looking around the room, rather than focusing on you, excuse yourself, and find someone else to talk to. Wandering eyes are a sign that he or she is not interested in you, and you're wasting your time continuing with the conversation.

Project an impression of confidence, and look as if you're having a good time.

Make good eye contact with others, and listen to what they have to say. If you show a genuine interest in others, you'll find that people will like you and want to get to know you better. Research that has been done on the length of eye contact shows that people who shared longer than usual eye contact during a casual conversation felt much more affectionate toward the other person than people who had less eye contact.[2]

Be aware of your personal space. Obviously, this doesn't apply in a crowded nightclub, but if someone you've recently met gradually gets closer and closer to you, you'll know he or she likes you.

The same thing applies to touching. If someone touches you in a friendly manner, and repeats the touching later on, you'll know he or she fancies you. Groping is a different matter entirely. Someone who gropes you all night is interested in taking you home for one thing only. This is fine, if that's what you're looking for, too. However, if you're looking for a potential relationship, a few gentle touches is more promising than a full-on grope. Men are usually happy to be touched by women. However, women are not as keen on being touched by men they've only just met.

Once you've started a conversation with someone who interests you, try to stand at a forty-five degree angle to him or her. This is an open and friendly position. Standing directly facing someone you've just met can be intimidating to some people.

Honesty

It's important to be honest when meeting someone new. I used to know a man who always told women that he was an airline pilot. He thought they'd be more likely to let him seduce them if they thought that was what he was, rather than the office worker that he happened to be. This might work on one-time encounters, but any long-term relationship based on dishonesty will inevitably fail.

The real secret in looking for a partner is to be yourself. Be honest. As the relationship develops, share more and more of yourself. Use the techniques in this chapter to meet people, and remain confident that sooner or later you'll find the right person for you.

Love or Lust

Psychologists have conducted experiments to see if it's possible to determine if two people on a first date were in love or lust. Gian Gonzaga and his colleagues secretly videotaped couples talking about their first date and then questioned them about it, asking them if the discussion was more about love than lust, or vice versa. The videotapes showed that when the couple decided the discussion was more about love, that the couple leaned toward each other, smiled, and nodded. Couples who decided the conversation was more about lust were more likely to lick their lips and to stick out their tongues.[3] It could be a good idea to see if your first date companion is leaning forward, or licking his or her lips.

Sustaining a Relationship

It's all very well spending time and energy finding the right partner, but once you've found him or her, you need to make sure the relationship becomes a permanent one. Like me, you've probably known a number of couples who appear to be made for each other. However, some of these apparent dream relationships fail to last. Obviously, every relationship is different, and what appears to be a perfect relationship to an outsider might feel like the opposite for the two people involved.

There are a number of factors to a successful, long-lasting relationship. These include:

- Loving each other, and expressing this in words and deeds
- Being committed to the relationship

- Being each other's best friend
- Being faithful, tolerant, and forgiving
- Devoting quality time to the relationship
- Trusting each other
- Communicating with each other

Entire books could be written about each of these. The only one we're concerned about here is the last one: communication. There must be good communication for the relationship to last, and this involves both nonverbal and spoken communication.

Laughter

There is usually plenty of laughter inside a happy relationship. Everyone experiences ups and downs in life, so there are bound to be tears at times, also. However, the ability to make the other person laugh and feel happy is vital.

Your eyebrows should rise, and your eyes open wide, when you greet your partner. The smiles need to be genuine, for the most part. There will always be times when one of you does something silly, and the other might smile, but not mean it. However, most of the smiles you share should be happy, genuine smiles involving the eyes as well as the mouth.

Hugging

Everyone loves to be hugged by someone they love. Hold your partner close, face to face, navel to navel, and hug him or her as if you really mean it. Hugs can reveal the state of a relationship.

If the hug is confined to the head and shoulders, and does not include the rest of the body, the sexual attraction has gone from the relationship.

There are significant relationship issues, especially concerning intimacy, if one partner always hugs the other from behind.

There are likely to be sexual problems if the hugs last only a matter of seconds.

These problems can all be resolved as long as the two people still love each other.

Touching

People who are in love touch each other all the time, as they enjoy being physically close. It's a sign of problems in the relationship if one person raises a shoulder to subconsciously fend the other person off.

Usually, when this occurs, the couple will tend to lean away from each other, and to increase the physical distance between them. A number of photographs of Prince Charles and Princess Diana show these postures, and clearly demonstrate the problems they were having in their relationship.

Walking

A happy couple will walk side by side. Depending on where they are, and what they're doing, they're likely to hold hands, or alternatively the woman may rest her hand on the man's arm. Often, and without knowing it, they'll synchronize their steps, too.

It's a sign of problems in the relationship when a couple walk separately, with one walking a number of paces behind the other. Subconsciously, the person in front is distancing him- or herself from the other.

Mirroring

Happy couples mirror each other all the time without realizing it. Deliberate mirroring is a useful technique in a sales situation, but is not necessary in a good relationship, as it happens automatically.

Time to Leave

Everyone dreams of finding the right person and living happily ever after. Unfortunately, this doesn't happen in many cases. In the United States, it's estimated that between 40 and 50 percent of all first marriages end in divorce, and up to 60 percent of second marriages end the same way.[4]

Every relationship experiences ups and downs, and if the couple are unable to resolve their problems it's often better for them to separate, rather than continue living in a state of stress and constant disagreement. If you want the relationship to survive, seek professional help before the situation gets totally beyond repair.

There are both verbal and nonverbal signs that it's time the relationship came to an end. Verbal indications include yelling, screaming, verbal putdowns, demeaning words, curses, and frequent arguments.

Nonverbal signs include one partner stabbing a finger toward the other person's face or chest. There can be no respect left after this. In fact, this is a serious, potentially dangerous sign, as the next step could be physical violence.

Another negative sign is when one person stands inside the other person's space with hands on hips and a snarling, angry expression on his or her face.

It's a danger sign if one person rolls his or her eyes, and/or sighs loudly while the other person is talking. This is especially the case if it's done in public, as well as in private.

Another rude and discourteous sign is for one partner to make faces and rude gestures while the other person is talking. This can be done openly, or behind the speaker's back.

Relationship breakups are stressful and difficult for everyone involved. Hopefully, over time, everyone involved learns and grows from the experience. Life itself is a learning experience, and we have opportunities to grow and develop every day. In the next chapter we'll look at how body language can help you on this path.

The human body is the best picture of the human soul.
—LUDWIG WITTGENSTEIN

chapter ten

BODY LANGUAGE FOR SELF-IMPROVEMENT

Your increasing knowledge of body language will help you in many ways. Other people will find you more approachable, and your dealings with others will become smoother and more successful.

You can use your body language skills to charm, captivate, and influence others. To do this, of course, you need to feel confident. Paying attention to your body language will help you feel in control in every type of situation.

When you feel confident, your posture reflects this. You'll automatically stand tall, make open postures, have good eye contact, smile genuinely at appropriate times, and avoid unnecessary movements. Your shoulders will be parallel to the shoulders of the person you're talking to. You won't look down when you break eye contact, as you know this makes you appear submissive. You'll breathe slowly and deeply, using your stomach and diaphragm. If you're feeling anxious, you can increase your confidence by breathing slowly, and altering your body language to portray a more confident posture.

You can do this for anything you wish. If you find yourself in a tense or stressful situation, deliberately slow down your breathing, stand or sit with an open posture, hold your head up high, and look directly at the person or people you're dealing with.

You can also use affirmations. Affirmations are short positive statements that relate to whatever it is you desire. They are always phrased in the present tense, as if you already had the quality you are seeking. You can say them, silently or out loud, whenever you wish. "I am confident," "I am calm and relaxed," and "I am successful" are all examples of affirmations. Interestingly, affirmations work, whether you believe in them or not.

You should repeat your affirmation as often as you can, and you'll find your body language changing to reflect your words. You can say affirmations to yourself whenever you wish. I often say them (silently) while waiting in line. I say them out loud when I'm driving in my car. Another good time to say them is while lying in bed at night waiting for sleep, and again as soon as you wake up in the morning.

By repeating your affirmations as often as you can, you'll influence your thoughts. As your mind can hold only one thought at a time, your affirmations effectively kick out any negative thoughts you may have been thinking. Thoughts contain energy. When you fill your mind with positive affirmations, you'll gradually become the person you want to be. This is an example of the old saying—that we become what we think about.

Once you've started looking the part, you need to start acting as if you already possess the qualities you desire. This isn't hard to do, as once you adopt the body language of someone who, for instance, is confident, you'll immediately start feeling confident. You may have reversals along the way. Whenever this happens, assume the desired posture, and start again. If you continue to do this, you'll reach a stage in which you feel confident most of the time.

It can be a good idea to sit down quietly and visualize a meeting or other event you're about to attend. In your mind's eye, picture yourself exactly as you wish to be. Notice your powerful, yet open, posture, and see yourself interacting with the other people present in a friendly, confident manner.

Eye Contact

Many people find it hard to make good eye contact with others. This is usually due to shyness, low self-esteem, and a lack of confidence. Unfortunately, people who fail to make good eye contact are considered negatively, and people might think you're dishonest or a snob.

If making good eye contact is hard for you, start by practicing looking at your eyes in a mirror when you're on your own. This should be easy to do, as you know you're gazing into your own eyes. However, this is just the first stage. Once you can look steadily into your own eyes for at least a minute, ask a trusted friend for help. Tell him or her about your problem, and ask if you could look into his or her eyes for as long as you can. If the person is a true friend, he or she will be happy to help.

Sit down, facing each other, and see if you can gaze into each other's eyes for at least thirty seconds. When you reach the stage of doing this with no difficulty, see if you can extend the time to one minute.

After this, it's time to practice with strangers. There is a large group of people in society who would love to exchange eye contact with you. Walk through any large store and make eye contact with the salespeople as you walk past. You'll find they'll be delighted to exchange a brief greeting with you. There's another benefit from doing this. As part of their training, they've been told to smile at potential customers, and this gives you the opportunity to smile back at them. If you're shopping for something, enlist the help of a salesperson. This gives you the chance to interact with a stranger. You'll have an opportunity to practice making good eye contact, while receiving help and recommendations on whatever it is you are planning to buy.

Once you become experienced at making eye contact with sales staff, expand this to other strangers whom you interact with in your everyday life. Make eye contact with your server when you go out for dinner. Do the same when you get your hair cut. You might exchange a few words with someone who is waiting for the same bus or train as you. You'll find many opportunities to make eye contact with people everywhere you go.

Once you reach this stage, you'll be making better eye contact with people, and it will cease to be a problem.

Put More Expression in Your Eyes

Many people go through life without showing much emotion in their eyes. While you're looking into your eyes in the mirror, see how many different expressions you can show in your eyes. You'll be able to indicate enthusiasm, surprise, awe, happiness, sincerity, humor, sadness, anger, empathy, skepticism, flirtatiousness, courage, and much more. Once you've experimented with these, ask your partner to try to read the different expressions you can create with your eyes.

Another good way to practice this is to allow your eyes to express every emotion you feel when you're watching a program on television.

Once you feel confident with the animation you can reveal through your eyes, put this skill into practice. People will read your emotions in your eyes, and will react favorably to them. You'll find that almost invariably they'll start revealing more of their feelings back to you through their eyes.

Smiling

A surprising number of people find it hard to smile. In actuality, they do smile, but it is either miniscule, or so brief that other people fail to see it. Often these people feel that they're smiling broadly, and are surprised when someone tells them they're not.

An attorney friend of mine told me recently that he finds it hard to smile. He has a permanently dour expression on his face, and someone had asked him why he was looking so sad. This made him check his face in the mirror, and he realized that although he was perfectly happy and contented, he looked extremely sad. I suggested that he rectify this by smiling more often.

"I just can't do it," he told me. "When I deliberately smile, it feels forced and unnatural. I'm convinced it makes me look evil."

I assured him that I'd seen him smile on many occasions, and he certainly didn't look evil. I suggested he return to his mirror and experiment with a variety of different smiles.

"Make some big smiles," I told him. "And then make some small ones. Make some sexy smiles, and then try some sarcastic ones. Do a bit of leering, and make a few big grins. And be sure to make some fake smiles, too, as I want you to see and feel how different they are to genuine smiles. Finish off by laughing at yourself in the mirror for as long as you can."

My friend tried this, much to the amusement of his wife. The first indication that he'd been practicing this exercise came a week later. We both belong to the same service club, and before dinner we have a drink and chat. He was standing in a group next to me, and I heard him laugh. I was so surprised, I turned to check that it was him. One of the other members had made a joke, and he'd laughed.

I was delighted, as it meant his problem had been solved. Although it's still rare to hear him laugh out loud, he smiles much more than he used to, and he's told me how much easier all his dealings with other people have become as a result.

Social Events

Many people hate the idea of going to a party, or other event, where they won't know many people. Fortunately, your body language skills will enable you to make a good impression. If you know you won't know many people, arrive early. This may sound like strange advice, but it will pay off. There won't be many other people there at that time, and you'll be able to talk with the other early arrivals. This means that by the time the party gets going, you'll already know a number of people, and they'll introduce you to their friends when they arrive. This is a good way to meet people if you find it hard to introduce yourself to complete strangers at a party.

Take a few deep breaths before walking into the room. Smile, hold your head up, and look confident. Once you're inside, pause and look around to see if you know anyone you wish to talk to. If there is, approach him or her only if the group the person is in looks as if they'd welcome a new addition. If the person is having an obviously serious conversation with someone else, he or she might not want to be interrupted. In this case, smile, make eye contact, and wave or say "hello" as you walk past.

Move into the center of the room. You're more likely to meet important people here, as the more timid souls will have gathered around the edges of the party. Look happy as you check to see if anyone is standing on his or her own. If there is, approach the person at an angle, smile, make eye contact, and make a casual remark. If you walk directly toward a stranger, he or she might feel threatened and uncomfortable. It's also important to take the initiative, and not be concerned about making the first approach. Chances are, the other person will be relieved to chat with you, rather than feel uncomfortable standing on his or her own.

If you find something in common, you might chat with this person for several minutes. If there's no connection, excuse yourself and find someone else to talk with.

With your ready smile and open posture, you'll meet some interesting new people, and may also catch up with friends.

Saying Goodbye

Saying goodbye is something that deserves thought, as it's the impression that people you've been spending time with are left with once you are gone. A good farewell is just as important in a casual encounter as it is in a business meeting, or a conversation on the phone. When people are in a hurry to get away, they sometimes forget to say their farewells graciously and sincerely.

Farewells shouldn't be rushed. Exchange a few pleasantries, and use a warm tone of voice. Lengthen your eye contact slightly, smile, and make physical contact with a handshake, hug, or any other farewell gesture that's appropriate for the situation.

Although we've mentioned it briefly in passing, we've left one of the most useful aspects of body language until the end. This is determining whether or not someone is lying. This important aspect of body language—lying and deceit—is the subject of the next chapter.

It is sometimes necessary to lie damnably
in the interests of the nation.
—HILAIRE BELLOC

chapter eleven

LIES AND DECEPTION

Both men and women lie, but they lie about different things. Men frequently lie when they try to convince others that they're more successful or fascinating than they actually are. Women frequently lie to protect the feelings of others, and to help people feel better about themselves. Jerald Jellison, social psychologist at the University of Southern California, believes we are being lied to about two hundred times a day.[1]

It's not always possible to tell if someone is lying to you. Some people are extremely good at lying to others, and show very little in the way of leakage. A large number of research studies show that most people are able to detect deliberate lying just over 50 percent of the time. This gives liars a huge advantage, as they know they'll be able to get away with their lies almost half of the time.

I know someone who tells lies even when it would be easier to say the truth. He leads a Walter Mitty type of existence, and regularly fantasizes about his life and what he's doing. Even when he's not lying, whatever story he tells is exaggerated to the nth degree. He's insecure, and does this to bolster his ego and self-esteem. I've known him for more than forty years, and am convinced he believes his lies while he's telling them. Consequently, it's rare to see any body language leakage. Because of this, someone who met him for the first time would believe his stories, as he is such a good liar.

Fortunately, most people are not very good at lying, and their deception can be read in their body language. When you're questioning someone whom you think is lying, make sure you have a clear view of his or her face, body, and legs. By doing this, you'll be more likely to spot incongruent actions. As always, you need to look for a cluster of gestures.

Mirroring

Mirroring can be found anywhere where people are getting along well with each other. It's a well-known method of gaining rapport with others. In fact, it's almost too well known, as it's even taught on dating sites. Most people who do it consciously give themselves away, as they become self-conscious or make it overly obvious what they're doing.

Interestingly, liars do not usually mirror the other person's body language. If you lean forward, for instance, he or she is likely to pull back. Consequently, the absence of mirroring can be a clue that the person is suffering from stress, and may well be lying.

Awkward Body Language

Someone who is not used to lying is likely to give him- or herself away by either trying not to make any gestures with his or her arms and legs, or alternatively make gestures that appear awkward.

Someone who is lying is likely to fidget, as this helps him or her handle the stress created by the lie. Tapping fingers, restless feet, wringing the hands, and toe tapping are indications of stress and anxiety.

Breathing

Telling lies is stressful for most people. Consequently, it's common for liars to take a deep breath and release it quickly. They do this because the sudden stress causes the body's autonomic nervous system to move into high gear. Taking a deep breath helps provide oxygen to the blood, and this helps relieve the stress.

Skin Color

Many people, myself included, flush when telling a lie. The problem with this, is that as soon as you become aware that you're blushing, the situation gets worse and your face becomes even redder. This is more noticeable in fair-skinned people, but people of all hues notice a rush of blood to the skin's surface when they're fabricating a story.

Perspiration

Stress affects people in different ways. Many people start to perspire when they tell a lie. Beads of perspiration start forming on the person's upper lip and then appear on his or her forehead. The person will wipe the sheen of sweat off his or her forehead, which is also a sign of deception.

Liars frequently get sweaty hands, too. They'll then wipe their hands against their clothing in an attempt to make them dry.

Perspiration caused by stress appears regardless of the room temperature. Because they start feeling warm, liars may have to loosen their collars and adjust other items of clothing to help them feel cooler again. These are all signs of deception.

Shaking

Because of the increase in muscle tension, some liars start to shake and feel unsteady. This is caused by a fear of being caught out in telling a lie. People who start shaking in this way might, for instance, find it hard to raise a cup of coffee to their lips, as their hands and arms feel out of control.

Muscle Twitch

Involuntary muscle twitches, especially in the temples, cheeks, and eyelids, are another sign of extreme stress and can be a sign that the person is lying or withholding valuable information. These twitches usually appear on one side of the person's face.

Asymmetry

Any gestures or expressions that do not occur evenly on both sides of the face could be a sign of deception. A lop-sided smile, one flared nostril, and a one-shoulder shrug are examples of this. Genuine emotions are usually revealed on the face symmetrically. The one exception to this is contempt, in which one side of the mouth is curled.

Micro-Expressions

Micro-expressions, the fleeting expressions that cross the face in a fraction of a second, provide valuable clues as to how someone feels about someone or something. As they're almost impossible to control, they're a valuable clue for anyone looking for signs of deception.

Posture

The posture of liars usually fits in to one of two types. The first type tilt their heads to one side, conceal their hands, fidget, shrug their shoulders, shuffle their feet, and rock backward and forward. Their eyes appear furtive, and blink rapidly.

Interestingly enough, the second type do almost the opposite. They hardly move at all. They stand or sit in a rigid, fixed manner. Even their gaze is unmoving and direct. If sitting, their hands rest on their laps and do not move.

However, habitual liars won't fit into either of these. They'll appear relaxed, smile readily, make good eye contact, and will want to get physically close to you. Once they suspect you're onto them, they'll start comforting themselves by touching themselves in various ways. They might, for instance, stroke their hair, rub their hands together, or cross their arms. They're also likely to expose the palms of their hands face up in a pleading gesture, as if begging you to believe them.

Avoiding Physical Contact

Liars tend to avoid physical contact when lying. They may stand slightly farther away from the person they are lying to than they normally do.

Stress

Inexperienced liars often suffer from stress when forced into telling a lie. They may experience an increased heart rate, breathlessness, shaking, and sweating. Their faces may become flushed, or perhaps do the opposite and turn pale. There could be a change in how they speak. They could speak louder or softer, or may find it hard to concentrate enough to put words together. They may become more emotional, and appear irrational.

The best way to deal with people in this state is to take a few slow, deep breaths yourself, and speak to them calmly and quietly. If necessary, suggest they take several deep breaths themselves. Offer a seat and a glass of water, and talk to them quietly until they calm down.

Stress can turn to aggression. If this happens, remain as calm and relaxed as you can, and speak quietly. Keep your posture open. If you are standing or sitting directly facing each other, change position to one that is less confrontational. If you are both standing, suggest that you sit down to discuss the problem. Listen carefully to what the angry person has to say. Don't interrupt him or her, and use body language to show that you're listening. When the person has finished speaking, respond in a calm manner. Make good eye contact, but be careful not to aggravate the situation by staring into his or her eyes for too long at a time.

Head

Small, involuntary movements of the head provide useful clues about possible deception. If someone tells you he or she loves you, but at the same time his or her head is moving from side to side to indicate "no," the head movement will be correct. Likewise, if someone says, "I did not talk to her," while at the same time slightly nodding his or her head, the head movement will be correct.

Another sign of possible deception occurs when someone who up to that point had been making good eye contact, turns his or her head away while speaking.

Many liars nod frequently when they're telling lies. This is done in an attempt to get the other person to accept the lie.

Forehead

The forehead and upper lip are the first place where a sheen of sweat gathers to indicate the degree of stress someone is under. This can be a sign that the person is lying.

Another indication occurs if the forehead rises to indicate surprise. It's possible he or she is surprised at being found out.

Eyes

People find it hard to look at others while telling a lie. This is not surprising as the eyes can unwittingly give away huge amounts of information. The person's eyes might blink more rapidly than usual while telling a lie. Conversely, they may do the complete opposite, and the person might use an unblinking stare, and refuse to break eye contact. A higher blink rate is caused by stress, but many liars are able to lower their blink rate. Habitual liars have no qualms about lying and consequently suffer no stress or have any fears about being found out. Dr. Samantha Mann, a psychologist at Portsmouth University, found that when suspects were interviewed by the police, they had more pauses in their speech, and blinked 18.5 times a minute. When they were telling the truth they blinked at an average rate of 23.6 times a minute.[2]

O. J. Simpson had a low blink rate when he was on trial for murdering his wife and Ron Goldman. Bill Clinton also had a low blink rate when he told the world he did not have a sexual relationship with Monica Lewinsky.[3] In contrast to this, former U.S. senator John Edwards blinked rapidly when he denied he was having an affair.[4]

Some people even close their eyes while telling a lie. This is to prevent the listener from seeing the truth revealed inside his or her eyes.

Some liars squint and frown when being questioned about a possible deception. Their eyes will glare at the accuser, angry that their words are being questioned.

If someone is caught telling a lie, the eyes will open wide and the white of the eyes will be visible above the iris, the colored part of the eye.

It's a sign of discomfort if someone suddenly changes the direction of his or her gaze. This can be a sign of lying.

Most people look down when they lie, get caught lying, or feel guilty about something they've done. They do this to avoid seeing the other person's anger, disappointment, or look of hurt.

Some men will rub their eyes while telling a lie. Women are more inclined to gently rub immediately below their eyes. Both of these are subconscious attempts to hide their eyes, so they can "see no evil."

The pupils constrict when people lie. There is no way of preventing this from happening, but skilled liars try to sit or stand in positions where their eyes are out of direct light. Many liars, as well as gamblers and negotiators, wear dark glasses to conceal the involuntary actions of the eyes.

Nose

The most common indication that someone may be lying is touching, scratching, or pulling on the nose. When someone tells a lie, the stress causes the capillaries of the nose to expand because of increased blood flow to the area. As children, we learned that Pinocchio's nose grew every time he told a lie. He wasn't alone, as the increased blood flow causes everyone's nose to temporarily expand when they're telling a lie. In addition to this, the mucous membranes dry up, causing discomfort and consequent itching.

Ear

Instead of scratching their nose, some people scratch or pull on an ear when they're telling lies.

The Mouth

It can be a sign of deception when someone's upper lip starts to perspire. This is especially the case if the temperature is not hot enough to cause the person to sweat.

Children cover their mouths when telling a lie. Most people learn to control this as they reach adulthood, but a surprising number of people bring their hands to their mouths when telling a lie. Sometimes the hands get diverted to the cheek, the side of the mouth, the ears, the chin, or nose. Touching the mouth is a common sign of anxiety, especially in people who feel nervous about something they've just said, or are about to say.

Lip licking can be a sign that someone is telling a lie. Increased stress causes the saliva in the mouth to dry up when people tell a lie, and they need to lick their lips to provide more saliva.

Some people appear to swallow their lies, and this can be seen by tension in the throat muscles. In men, the Adam's apple will bob up and down when this occurs. Constant licking of the lips and frequent swallowing usually appear together, and are an excellent indication that the person is lying. Frequent throat clearing, if accompanied by other indications, can be a sign that the person is lying.

Many liars wipe their mouths with an open palm. This is almost as if they are wiping any residual traces of the lie away.

Biting the lower lip can also be a sign that the person in lying. However, this needs to be read in context. Many people bite their lower lips while thinking about something.

A lopsided, false smile is often a sign of deception. If you're trying to determine if someone is lying or telling the truth, look at the person's eyes when he or she smiles. Many people find it impossible to give a genuine smile when they're lying. It's been estimated that only one person in ten can successfully fake a true smile. This is because it's difficult to control the fine muscles around the eyes.[5]

Voice

Many liars give themselves away with their voices. The pitch might change slightly, or the voice might sound strained or tremble when they speak. They may need to clear their throat frequently, too.

Jaw

A tightly clenched jaw is another example of what the body does when someone is under stress. Often it's accompanied by an involuntary muscle twitch.

Adam's Apple

Many people have a need to lubricate their throats and swallow before telling a lie. This is easier to detect in men, as their Adam's apple moves and gives them away.

Hands

As a rule, people expose the palms of their hands when telling the truth. Often, people hide their hands when lying. They might sit on them, place them deep into their pockets, or conceal them behind a desk. They might even curl the fingers into a fist to hide the fingers.

They might clasp their hands, hold tightly to a table or arm rests, or clutch their upper arms, to prevent the hands from moving. The tension they're experiencing is often clearly visible in the hands.

Many liars give a hand shrug, which occurs when the hands are held out and rotated to expose the palms. It's an interesting gesture, as it's almost as if the liar is trying to gain sympathy because he or she has been caught lying.

Children cover their mouths with their hands after telling a lie. Adults have learned not to do this, but often feel a need to bring a hand to their face. Instead of covering their mouth, they might rub their nose or ear, or touch another part of the face.

Abdomen

Some liars experience a sudden pain in their abdomen caused by stress. This is usually accompanied by an urgent need to visit the bathroom. In extreme cases, the pain causes people to feel nauseous, and even vomit.

Feet Movement

Frequently, people stop all movement above the waist when they're telling a lie. They'll look directly at the person they're lying to, without blinking. Their elbows are kept close to their sides, and the hands may be clasped.

However, although they can keep the top half still, they find it almost impossible to prevent their legs and feet from moving around. They may continually cross and uncross their legs, shuffle their feet, or tap their toes.

How to Lie

We were all brought up to believe that lying is bad, and we should always tell the truth. As a result of this, most people feel guilty when they tell a lie, and these feelings are revealed in our body language.

A British study determined that men lie approximately six times a day, while women lie three times.[6] This study of two thousand people also revealed that the most common lie is one I've said myself: "Nothing's wrong, I'm fine." People lie for many reasons. It might be an attempt to gain respect. Someone I know tells people he's a car salesman when he actually spends his days grooming cars for resale. Most people will lie to spare someone else's feelings. A man could be in serious trouble if his wife asks him if her new dress makes her backside look fat, and he thinks it does. Men and women frequently lie to each other when they first meet, as they want to create a good impression. Most of these lies are relatively harmless, and help life go more smoothly. As these "white lies" are generally said with good motives, it's important that other people believe them.

As you know, it's hard to lie successfully, as your autonomic nervous system conspires against you, causing blushing, sweating upper lips, foreheads, and palms, dry mouth, tickly throat, and an itchy nose. It takes a great deal of effort and practice to control all of this. This is why many people are found out by changes in their speech patterns. They may talk slowly, make mistakes in their speech, or take longer than usual to respond to a question. Their movements also slow down. They find it hard, or impossible, to mirror the other person's posture. It's hard to speak and move naturally when you're so busy trying to control everything else.

Assuming that you have your autonomic nervous system under control, here are some other things you need to be aware of if you're going to tell a lie.

If possible, prepare your lie in advance. This gives you the opportunity to determine exactly what you're going to say, and how you're going to say it. Practice by visualizing yourself saying the lie. Notice the posture you assume, and change it if necessary. See yourself saying the lie and having it accepted by the other person. Then see yourself leaving the situation knowing that your lie has been accepted.

When it comes to telling the lie, don't increase eye contact. If you do, and especially if you also fail to blink, the other person will probably notice the change. Children tend to look away when they're telling a lie. Consequently, adult liars think that increasing the amount of eye contact will make them more believable. This is not the case.

Keep your body posture as normal as possible. Liars tend to stiffen their bodies, and look more rigid than usual. If you are normally animated, the sudden change will be a strong giveaway that you're lying. Even if your normal gestures are restrained, anyone who knows you will be able to detect the changes in your body.

When people are stressed, their breathing changes and they make frequent, shallow breaths that can give them away. To avoid this, take several slow, deep breaths before entering the place where you'll be telling the lie. Exhale before saying the lie. Doing this allows you to release tension before you speak. This also makes you sound normal, as the pitch of your voice can change when you're nervous and under pressure.

Speak normally. Long pauses, or no pauses at all, can be considered a sign of deception. Stuttering, or overuse of "um…" and "er…" can also lead to people questioning what you say.

Don't fidget. Liars tend to move their arms and legs a great deal. The hands might clasp the arms for a few moments, and then disappear into the pockets, and then one will reappear and touch the face, and so on. Touching anywhere on the face, but especially the nose and mouth, are indications of possible deception. Instead of fidgeting, keep your arms by your sides, or on your lap. Excessive arm and hand movements, as well as a total lack of them, make people suspicious.

Make modest use of open palm gestures. Open palms are a sign of openness, honesty, and integrity. Most people instinctively trust people who make open palm gestures. People who conceal their palms could be telling lies. Consequently, if you're telling a lie, expose the open palm, but do so sparingly. If you overdo it, it will raise suspicions, especially if you aren't in total control of all your autonomic nervous system responses.

Keep your hands out of your pockets, as you want them to be visible. Your hand gestures should be as natural as possible. When people are stressed they're inclined to use repetitive comforting gestures such as touching their neck, stroking their hair, or wringing their hands, to reduce the stress. These gestures all reveal the stress they're trying to conceal, and are likely to be considered signs of deception.

If you must do something with your hands, allow the tips of your thumb and first finger to touch. The touching sensation will help reduce stress, and if you need to, you can move your thumb and forefinger slightly to reduce it even further. Actors often do this before walking onto the stage, to reduce stage fright.

Whenever possible, experienced liars hide the lower half of their bodies behind a desk. This conceals any involuntary leg and foot movements. In addition, the desk acts as a barrier that helps the liar to feel more comfortable.

You can't prevent your pupils from constricting when telling a lie. The best you can do is to keep your face in a place that makes it hard for other people to see into your eyes.

Liars sometimes give themselves away at the end of the questioning. Once it's all over, an expression of relief crosses their face. Avoid this, and you may find you've got away with your lie this time.

Use nonverbal communication to SOFTEN the hard-line
position of others: S = Smile O = Open Posture F = Forward Lean
T = Touch E = Eye Contact N = Nod.
—ANONYMOUS

CONCLUSION

You now know that actions speak much louder than words. A famous quote, attributed to Ralph Waldo Emerson (1803–1882), the American poet and essayist, goes: "What you are speaks so loudly, I cannot hear what you say." This shows that people will judge you by your actions. Small acts of courtesy are often remembered for a lifetime. Your body language reflects exactly who you are, as your actions come directly from your innermost thoughts.

This is why so many figures of speech relate to body language. People flush with embarrassment, shrug their shoulders in indifference, tap their fingers with impatience, raise an eyebrow in disbelief, grit their teeth, stiffen their upper lip, tremble with rage, and freeze with fright.

You now have a better understanding of how all of us reveal ourselves to others without saying a word. You may have modified your behavior, or made some changes to how you stand, walk, and sit to convey what you want others to see. Everyone adjusts their behavior to try to fit in with what is required at the time. Someone who is petrified about giving a speech, for instance, will try to look calm and confident as he or she steps onto the stage.

You'll also be paying attention to the body language of others, both on television and in real life, and starting to understand the motivations and feelings of other people. It can be very useful to see a situation from the other person's point of view. It enables you to make better judgments, be more empathetic, and lead a more balanced and harmonious life.

If you find it hard to read a particular person's body language, go with your feelings and impressions. Your initial gut reaction will usually be right, even though you may not know logically why something feels right or wrong. I learned years ago to follow my intuition whenever logic indicated one direction and my intuition another. My intuition is almost always right. Yours will be, too.

Naturally, you should use logic also, based on what you've learned about nonverbal communication. If you still find the person's body language hard to interpret, make the gesture yourself and see what it feels like. This will help you gain insight into what the person was experiencing as he or she made the gesture.

It takes time to become good at reading body language, though, as there's a great deal to learn and understand. Your current body language has been developed over a lifetime, and it takes time and effort to change. You're bound to slip back into old patterns of behavior every now and again. This doesn't matter. Simply remind yourself of the changes you wish to make, and continue working on them until they become a natural part of your everyday behavior. You'll also find your confidence and self-esteem will increase as you discover you can feel at ease in every type of situation using your body language skills.

You're also likely to surprise people who've known you for a long time. Some of them may not like the changes you're making. When this occurs, tell them why you're making the changes you are, and ask them to help you by telling you privately about any lapses you might make.

The best way to make changes in your body language is to focus on one aspect at a time. You might start with your posture, for instance, and then move on to eye contact, and what you do with your hands and arms. You'll start noticing the reactions of others to these changes almost immediately, and this will encourage you to continue making changes until you become the person you want to be. Each small change will increase your confidence, and make the next change that much easier to do. Changing your body language will make a huge difference ino your life. You'll get on better with others, feel more confident and in control, become more approachable, and be more understanding and tolerant of others. You'll also become much more charismatic. People will want to spend time with you, as they'll feel comfortable and at ease in your company. You'll be more influential, self-possessed, and secure. It's a journey that enables you to make the most of your opportunities, and achieve everything you desire.

Fortunately, it's easy to practice body language. People watching is a fascinating activity, and you'll be able to observe people's body language everywhere you go. You can learn a great deal about body language by spending an hour or two in an airport or a shopping mall.

It can be fascinating to watch the body language of politicians, sports stars, and actors on television. However, these people are likely to have had training in how to present themselves. It can be even more useful to watch the body language of people in the news, or on reality programs. I enjoy watching television with the sound turned off, and can usually tell what's going on from the nonverbal signals the different people are using.

Knowledge of body language has enriched and enhanced my life in many ways. If you continue to work at it, I know it will do the same for you.

Take care of your body. It's the only place you have to live.
—JIM ROHN

appendix

HEALTH AND
BODY LANGUAGE

Now that you can read other people's body language and have made any desired changes to your own nonverbal communication, it's time to pay attention to the messages your body is telling you.

Our bodies constantly send out messages that can be read by others. People who know nothing about nonverbal communication are largely unaware of these messages. Our bodies also send us silent messages, telling us when something is wrong from a health point of view. Again, people who are not familiar with this are largely unaware of the possible emotional reasons behind their pain.

A tension headache caused by stress and pressure is a common experience, and most people take an aspirin to try to escape the stressful situation for a while. The headache is a message from the body telling us to get away from whatever is causing the stress.

Unfortunately, many people can't do this. If the stress is caused by a particular situation at work, it may not be possible to move away from the situation. The remedy is to find a new job or, if that's not possible, you'll need to learn how to handle the problem without becoming stressed.

As our bodies are delicate instruments that respond to everything that's going on in our lives, it's important to be aware of the connection between our emotional states and our physical symptoms. For many years, I worked as an osteopath and my clients were constantly amazed at how I could relate each vertebra in the spine to a specific problem. Lower back pain is often related to financial problems, for instance.

Often it seemed the person's body was silently giving me information that told me about his or her fears, beliefs, and unexpressed feelings. I quickly learned that many people did not want to discuss this. They wanted a cure for the immediate pain, but weren't prepared to deal with whatever caused it in the first place. Consequently, some of them became regular clients, because as long as they continued hanging on to negative emotions and fears, their bodies continued to send them messages that something was wrong by giving them back and neck pain.

We're meant to be fit and healthy. When we become ill, the most likely cause is an imbalance somewhere in the body, probably caused by suppressed emotions and a lack of self-love. Usually, our bodies have been trying to tell us about the problem, but we failed to listen. Because we didn't listen, the body then causes us to experience pain, and this forces us to do something about it.

Here are some of the signs your body may send to you, along with the possible cause of the problem.

- Headaches—Conflict, stress, pressure, and resentment.
- Migraines—Too much pressure on self, perfectionism.
- Eyes—Not wanting to see something. Glaucoma—inability to express emotions; cataracts—gloomy view of the future; long-sighted—looking ahead and ignoring the present; short-sighted—

inability to put things in perspective; blurred vision—loss of perspective.

- Ears—Not wanting to listen. Ignoring messages from the body.
- Neck—Rigid, controlling approach. Lack of flexibility.
- Throat—Inability to express one's inner self. Resisting change. Holding back.
- Shoulders—Carrying too heavy a load. Reluctance to let go.
- Back—Feeling unsupported, feeling sorry for self, overly serious approach to life. Lower back—financial pressure; middle back—accepting too many responsibilities; upper back—emotional problems, difficulties in giving and receiving love.
- Heart—Difficulty in giving and receiving love. Lack of joy in everyday life.
- Lungs—Suppressed grief, feeling not good enough, smothered.
- Stomach—Unwilling to accept new ideas. Unable to "stomach" something.
- Pancreas—Difficulty in expressing innermost thoughts and feelings.
- Liver—Problems with feelings and emotions.
- Bladder—Nervousness, apprehension, fear of letting go.
- Tailbone—Survival issues. Hanging on, unwillingness to let go.
- Hands—Problems in reaching out to others. Right hand—problems in giving; left hand—problems in receiving.
- Elbows—Inflexible approach to life. Resentment.
- Hips—Stubbornness and obstinacy.
- Legs—Unwilling to progress and move forward.
- Knees—Stubbornness, childhood pain and resentments.
- Ankles—Fear of sensuality and sexuality.
- Feet—Problems in staying grounded.

If someone has a sore knee, for instance, it might be caused by a resentment that began in childhood, but it may also have been caused by twisting it while playing a sport or making an unexpected movement. Some people claim that all pain has a psychological cause, and that the sore knee relates to a childhood problem no matter what caused it to occur. This may well be the case sometimes, but I don't agree that it is the cause of every instance of pain.

Exercise for Pain Relief

If you are suffering pain in any part of your body, you can ask it to help you understand what the problem is, and why you're experiencing it. It's a simple process that most people find relaxing and enjoyable.

Set aside at least thirty minutes, and make sure you won't be disturbed. The room should be reasonably warm, but not hot, and you should wear loose-fitting clothes. Sit in a comfortable chair, or lie down on the floor, if you wish. You might be able to do this exercise lying on a bed. I can't, as I fall asleep far too easily, and invariably drift off if I do this lying in bed. I don't have this problem when I lie down on the floor.

1. Take several slow deep breaths, holding each breath for a few seconds before exhaling. On each exhale, silently say, "Relax, relax, relax."

2. Focus on the toes of your left foot, and tell them to relax. You might feel a tingling sensation as they relax. Once the toes are relaxed, allow the relaxation to drift into your foot and up to your ankles. Repeat this with the right foot, until both feet feel completely relaxed.

3. Focus on your left foot again, and allow the relaxation to drift up your leg, over the knee and into your thigh. Again, repeat this with the right foot.

4. Allow the relaxation to drift up into your abdomen and chest. Take as long as you need to feel totally relaxed in these areas.

5. Allow the relaxation to drift down your left arm, all the way to the tips of your fingers. Repeat with the right arm.

6. Allow the relaxation to drift into your neck and face. Pay particular attention to the fine muscles around your eyes, and allow them to relax completely before allowing the relaxation to drift to the top of your head.

7. You're now completely relaxed. Mentally scan your body to see if any part is not fully relaxed. Focus on these areas until they relax.

8. Allow your attention to move to the part of your body that is experiencing pain. The relaxation exercise may have made the pain disappear temporarily, but you know where it is. While you're focusing on this part of your body, silently ask yourself, "Why am I experiencing the pain in my (the part of your body where the pain is)?" Let go of that thought, and enjoy the relaxation in your body. After a few seconds a thought may come into your mind that will help you clarify the reason for the pain. If this occurs, continue enjoying the relaxation for as long as you wish, and then move on to step 10.

9. If the answer doesn't come to you after a minute or two, ask the question again. Once you've done this, focus on the pleasant relaxation throughout your body. It's important that you don't stress or demand an answer. If the answer doesn't come to you while you're doing the relaxation exercise, it will come later. If the answer fails to come the second time you ask it, wait a minute or two, and ask again.

10. While you're in this peaceful, relaxed state, send healing to the affected part of your body. You can do this in a variety of ways. I like to visualize a pure, healing white light that enters my body

through the top of my head and sends healing to every part of my body, including the area where I'm experiencing pain. Sometimes, I visualize a warm sensation that completely surrounds the area and provides healing energy. On some occasions, I've visualized my guardian angel touching the area and sending divine healing to it. You might visualize the area of pain becoming smaller and smaller until it disappears. It makes no difference how you do it. The important part is to consciously send love and healing energy to the part of your body that needs it.

11. Continue enjoying the relaxation for as long as you wish, and then conclude the exercise by taking three slow deep breaths, opening your eyes, stretching, and then carrying on with your day. Have something to eat and drink shortly after you've finished this exercise.

While you were doing this exercise, you may have gained insights into why you're experiencing the pain. Many people do, but others don't. However, because of the exercise, the information you're seeking may pop into your head during the day, or you might receive it as soon as you wake up in the morning.

If necessary, repeat the exercise, but instead of asking a question, ask for a symbol that will help you understand why you're suffering pain. Alternatively, if the area involved is listed above, think about the key words associated with it, and see if they help provide you with the answer.

Your body will respond to your questions, but the answers may come when you're least expecting them. Be patient, and the answer will come.

Helping Others Control Stress

Stress builds up over a period of time, and sometimes other people are aware of the problem before the sufferer realizes it him- or herself.

There are a number of body language clues that can alert others to the problem.

The person may appear to be tense most of the time. He or she might show irritation by shrugging his or her shoulders, fidgeting, looking heavenward, or sighing. He or she might be unusually sensitive. He or she is likely to look listless and wear a hangdog expression most of the time. If the person is depressed, he or she might be slightly stooped. He or she might tremble when under pressure.

The stressed person will experience a variety of symptoms that may include tense muscles, an increased heart rate, indigestion, nausea, exhaustion, and sleep problems.

Often, the stressed person will not want to discuss his or her problems with others. If necessary, suggest counseling, medical help, or time off work. Be willing to spend time with the person, and to listen to whatever he or she has to say. Be helpful, caring, understanding, and empathetic.

NOTES

Chapter One

1. Mike Nicol, "Nelson Mandela's Warders" (Nelson Mandela Foundation, n.d.), http://www.nelsonmandela.org/images/uploads/Nelson_Mandelas_Warders.pdf.

2. This famous quote of Cary Grant can be found in many places, including *The New York Times*: http://www.nytimes.com/1988/11/03/arts/review-television-how-and-why-cary-grant-was-like-no-one-else.html.

3. Vittorio Gallese, Luciano Fadigo, Leonardo Fogassi, and Giacomo Rizzolatti, "Action Recognition in the Premotor Cortex." Article in *Brain*, Volume 119, Issue 2, 593–609 (Oxford: Oxford University Press, 1996). Available online at: http://brain.oxfordjournals.org/content/119/2/593.full.pdf+html.

Chapter Two

1. Jonathan Cole, *About Face* (Cambridge, MA: The MIT Press, 1998), 50.

2. Daniel Goleman, *Emotional Intelligence* (New York: Bantam Books, Inc., 1975), 13–20.

3. Eva Krumhuber, Antony S. R. Manstead, and Arvid Kappas, "Temporal Aspects of Facial Displays in Person and Expression Perception: The Effects of Smile Dynamics, Head-tilt, and Gender." Article in *Journal of Nonverbal Behavior*, 31:39–56 (Dordrecht, Netherlands: Springer Science + Business Media, LLC, 2007).

4. E. A. Haggard and K. S. Isaacs, "Micro-momentary Facial Expressions as Indicators of Ego Mechanisms in Psychotherapy." Article in *Methods of Research in Psychotherapy*, edited by L. A. Gottschalk and A. H. Auerbach, (New York: Appleton-Century-Crofts, 1966), 154–165. There are numerous accounts of this on the Internet, including: http://www.starpulse.com/news/index.php/2009/10/22/david_bowie_s_mismatched_eyes_were_the_r_1.

5. Desmond Morris, *The Naked Man* (London: Jonathan Cape, 2008), 64–65.

6. Paul Ekman, *Emotions Revealed* (New York: Henry Holt and Company, 2003), 14–15.

7. John Nolte, *The Human Brain: An Introduction to its Functional Anatomy* (Philadelphia: Mosby, Inc., 1999), 431–432.

8. Ken Cooper, *Nonverbal Communication for Business Success* (New York: AMACOM, 1979), 75.

9. Marianne LaFrance, *Lip Service: Smiles in Life, Death, Trust, Lies, Work, Memory, Sex and Politics* (New York: W. W. Norton & Company, 2011), XI.

10. Nathan A. Fox and Richard J. Davidson, "Electroencephalogram Asymmetry in Response to the Approach of a Stranger and Maternal Separation in 10-month-old Children." Article in *Developmental Psychology*, Vol 23 (2), March 1987, 233–240.

11. G. B. Duchenne de Boulogne (translated and edited by R. Andrew Cuthbertson), *The Mechanism of Human Facial Expression* (New York: Cambridge University Press, 1990), 277–279. (Originally published in French in 1862.)

12. E. Krumhuber, A. S. R. Manstead, and A. Kappas, "Temporal Aspects of Facial Displays in Person and Expression Perception. The Effects of Smile Dynamics, Head-Tilt and Gender." Article in *Journal of Nonverbal Behavior*, 31 (Springer Science and Business Media, 2007), 39–56. http://psych.cf.ac.uk/home2/anstead/2007_K,percent20M,percent20K,percent202007,percent20Journalpercent2

0ofpercent20nonverbalpercent20behavior,percent2031,percent20p39
.pdf.

13. Stanley Milgram, "Behavioral Study of Obedience." Article in
Journal of Abnormal and Social Psychology 67 (4), 1963, 371–378. A
fuller account of this experiment, and nineteen variations of it,
can be found in: Stanley Milgram, *Obedience to Authority: An Experi-
mental View* (New York: Harper & Row, Inc., 1974).

14. Stanley Milgram, "Behavioral Study of Obedience" (*The Journal of
Abnormal and Social Psychology*, Vol. 67, No 4, 1963), 375. This can
be found online at: www.columbia.edu/cu/psychology/terrace
/w1001/readings/milgram.pdf.

15. Roger E. Axtell, *Gestures: The Do's and Taboos of Body Language
Around the World* (New York: John Wiley & Sons, Inc., 1991), 72.

Chapter Three

1. Roger E. Axtell, *Gestures: The Do's and Taboos of Body Language
Around the World* (New York: John Wiley & Sons, Inc., Revised edition 1998), 46.

2. http://www.chevrolet.co.uk/experience-chevrolet/news/2010
/news/news-details2010-18.html.

3. Rosemary Pennington, "Shaking Hands in the Muslim World."
Article in *Muslim Voices* (December 24, 2009). http://muslimvoices
.org/shaking-hands-muslim-world/.

Chapter Six

1. Max A. Eggert, *Body Language for Business* (New York: Skyhorse
Publishing, 2012), 36–37.

2. Janine Willis and Alexander Todorov, "First Impressions: Making
Up Your Mind after a 100-Ms Exposure to a Face." Article in *Psychological Science* 17 (Thousand Oaks, CA: Sage Publications, July
2006), 592. http://pss.sagepub.com/content/17/7/592.abstract.

Chapter Seven

1. Tiffany Field, Miguel Diego, and Maria Hernandez-Reif, "Preterm Infant Massage Therapy: A Review" (*Infant Behavior Development*, April 2010, 33 [2]0, 115–124. http://www.ncbi.nlm.nih.gov /pmc/articles/PMC2844909/.

2. M. J. Hertenstein, D. Keltner, B. App, B.A. Bulleit, and A. R. Jaskola, "Touch Communicates Distinct Emotions." Article in *Emotion*, August 6 2006, (3): 528–533.

3. Nicolas Guéguen, "The Effect of a Woman's Incidental Tactile Contact on Men's Later Behavior." Article in *Social Behavior and Personality: An International Journal*, volume 38, number 2 (Scientific Journal Publishers, 2010), 257–266.

4. J. Guéguen and J. Fischer-Lokou, "Tactile Contact and Spontaneous Help: An Evaluation in a Natural Setting." Article in *Journal of Social Psychology*, December 2003, 143(6), 785–787.

5. http://www.tipping.org/tips/megatips.pdf.

6. R. G. Harper, A. N. Wiens, and J. D. Matarazzo, *Nonverbal Communication: The State of the Art* (New York: John Wiley & Sons, Inc., 1978), 297.

7. http://www.clivejames.com/pieces/dreaming/paul-keating.

8. Michael Thornton, "One's New Best Friend: The Queen, Michelle and the new touchy-feely protocol." Article in *MailOnline* (May 3, 2012). http://www.dailymail.co.uk/femail/article-1166490/Ones -new-best-friend-The-Queen-Michelle-new-touchy-feely-protocol .html.

Chapter Eight

1. http://www.zoominfo.com/#!search/profile/person?personId =101438980&targetid=profile.

2. J. Hanna, "Power Posing: Fake It Until You Make It." Article in *Harvard Business School Working Knowledge*, September 20, 2010.) http://hbswk.hbs.edu/item/6461.html.

3. Jeremy I. Skipper, Susan Goldin-Meadow, Howard C. Nusbaum, and Steven L. Small, "Speech-associated gestures, Broca's area, and the human mirror system." Article in *Brain and Language* 101 (3), 2007, 260–277. Available online at: http://www.ncbi.nlm.nih.gov/pmc/articles/PMC2703472/.

4. Brendan Marrocco, quoted in "Soldier Receives Double Arm Transplant and Eager to Live Independently" by Alex Dominguez. Article in *Time*, January 30, 2013.

Chapter Nine

1. Monica M. Moore, "Nonverbal Courtship Patterns in Women: Context and Consequences." Article in *Ethology and Sociobiology* 6 (New York: Elsevier Science, 1985), 237–247.

2. Joan Kellerman, James Lewis, and James D. Laird, "Looking and Loving: The Effects of Mutual Gaze on Feelings of Romantic Love." Article in *Journal of Research in Personality* 23:2 (New York: Elsevier, June 1989), 145–161.

3. G. C. Gonzaga, R. A. Turner, D. Keltner, B. C. Kampos, and M. Altemus. "Romantic Love and Sexual Desire in Close Bonds." Article in *Emotion*, 6 (2) (Washington. DC: Emotion, May 2006), 163–179.

4. "How Common Is Divorce and What Are the Reasons." Unattributed article (University of St. Augustine, n.d., http://www.divorce.usu.edu/files/uploads/Lesson3.pdf.

Chapter Eleven

1. Jerald Jellison, quoted in James Geary, "How to Spot a Liar." Article in *Time Magazine Europe*, March 13, 2000. http://www.time.com/time/world/article/0,8599,2051177,00.html.

2. Roger Dobson and Ed Habershon, "Liars Don't Blink: They Keep Still and Concentrate Hard." Article in *The Sunday Times* (London), March 19, 2006. Available online at: http://www.timesonline.co.uk/tol/news/uk/article742788.ece.

3. J. J. Teece, "Body Language of Criminals" (February 25, 2009), www.bowdoin.edu/visitors-friends/bowdoin-breakfast/pdf/1-body-language.pdf.

4. "How to Tell If Someone Is Lying." Unattributed article (September 8, 2009). http://abcnews.go.com/GMA/Books/story?id=574750&page=1.

5. Mary Suenwald, "The Physiology of Facial Expressions." Article in *Discover* (January 2005). http://discovermagazine.com/2005/jan/physiology-of-facial-expressions#.UT0_uhwQ6uo.

6. "Men Lie Six Times a Day, and Twice as Often as Women, Study Finds." Unattributed article in *The Daily Mail*, September 14, 2009. Available online at: http://www.dailymail.co.uk/news/article-1213171/Men-lie-times-day-twice-women-study-finds.html.

SUGGESTED READING

Ardrey, Robert. *The Territorial Imperative*. London: William Collins, 1967.

Argyle, Michael, and Mark Cook. *Gaze and Mutual Gaze*. Cambridge, UK: Cambridge University Press, 1976.

Axtell, Roger E. *Gestures: The Do's and Taboos of Body Language Around the World*. New York: John Wiley & Sons, Inc., 1991. Revised edition 1998.

Beattie, Geoffrey. *Visible Thought: The New Psychology of Body Language*. New York: Routledge, 2004.

Berne, Eric. *Games People Play*. New York: Grove Press, 1964.

Birdwhistell, R. L. *Kinesics and Context*. London: Allen Lane, 1971.

Borg, James. *Body Language: 7 Easy Lessons to Master the Silent Language*. Harlow, UK: Pearson Education Limited, 2008.

Colton, Helen. *The Gift of Touch: How Physical Contact Improves Communication, Pleasure and Health*. New York: Putnam Publishing Group, 1983.

Darwin, Charles. *The Expression of the Emotions in Man and Animals*. London: John Murray, 1872.

Eggert, Max A. *Body Language for Business*. New York: Skyhorse Publishing, 2012.

Ekman, Paul. *Telling Lies: Clues to Deceit in the Marketplace, Politics, and Marriage*. New York: W. W. Norton, Inc., 1991.

————. *Unmasking the Face: A Guide to Recognizing Emotions from Facial Expressions*. Englewood Cliffs, NJ: Prentice-Hall, 1975.

Fast, Julius. *Body Language*. London: Pan Books Limited, 1971.

————. *Body Language in the Workplace*. New York: Penguin Books, 1991.

Field, Tiffany. *Touch*. Cambridge, MA: MIT Press, 2003.

Hall, Edward T. *The Hidden Dimension: An Anthropologist Examines Humans' Use of Space in Public and in Private*. New York: Doubleday & Company, 1966.

Harper, R. G., A. N. Wiens, and J. D. Matarazzo. *Nonverbal Communication: The State of the Art*. New York: John Wiley & Sons, Inc., 1978.

Hay, Louise. *You Can Heal Your Life*. Carlsbad, CA: Hay House, Inc., 1984.

LaFrance, Marianne. *Lip Service: Smiles in Life, Death, Trust, Lies, Work, Memory, Sex and Politics*. New York: W. W. Norton & Company, 2011.

Lieberman, David J. *You Can Read Anyone: Never Be Fooled, Lied to, or Taken Advantage of Again*. Lakewood, NJ: Vitor Press, 2007.

Mehrabian, Albert. *Nonverbal Communication*. Piscataway, NJ: Transaction Publishers, 2007.

————. *Silent Messages: Implicit Communication of Emotions and Attitudes*. Belmont, CA: Wadsworth, 1971. Second edition 1981.

Meyer, Pamela. *Liespotting: Proven Techniques to Detect Deception*. New York: St. Martin's Press, 2010.

Morris, Desmond. *Bodywatching: A Field Guide to the Human Species*. London: Jonathan Cape Ltd., 1985.

————. *The Naked Man*. London: Jonathan Cape Ltd., 2008.

————. *The Naked Woman*. London: Jonathan Cape Ltd., 2004.

Morrison, Terri, and Wayne A. Conaway. *Kiss, Bow or Shake Hands: The Bestselling Guide to Doing Business in More Than 60 Countries*. Avon, UK: Adams Media, 2006.

Nierenberg, Gerard I., and Henry H. Calero. *How to Read a Person Like a Book*. New York: Pocket Books, 1971.

Pease, Allan. *Body Language: How to Read Others' Thoughts by Their Gestures*. Avalon Beach, Australia: Camel Publishing Company, 1981.

Ribbens, Geoff, and Greg Whitear. *Body Language*. London: Hodder Arnold, 2007.

Webster, Richard. *Face Reading Quick and Simple*. Woodbury, MN: Llewellyn Publications, 2012.

INDEX

H

I

J

K

To Write to the Author

If you wish to contact the author or would like more information about this book, please write to the author in care of Llewellyn Worldwide Ltd. and we will forward your request. Both the author and publisher appreciate hearing from you and learning of your enjoyment of this book and how it has helped you. Llewellyn Worldwide Ltd. cannot guarantee that every letter written to the author can be answered, but all will be forwarded. Please write to:

Richard Webster
℅ Llewellyn Worldwide
2143 Wooddale Drive
Woodbury, MN 55125-2989

Please enclose a self-addressed stamped envelope for reply,
or $1.00 to cover costs. If outside the U.S.A., enclose
an international postal reply coupon.

GET MORE AT LLEWELLYN.COM

Visit us online to browse hundreds of our books and decks, plus sign up to receive our e-newsletters and exclusive online offers.

- • Free tarot readings • Spell-a-Day • Moon phases
- • Recipes, spells, and tips • Blogs • Encyclopedia
- • Author interviews, articles, and upcoming events

GET SOCIAL WITH LLEWELLYN

Find us on
Facebook
www.Facebook.com/LlewellynBooks

Follow us on

www.Twitter.com/Llewellynbooks

GET BOOKS AT LLEWELLYN

LLEWELLYN ORDERING INFORMATION

Order online: Visit our website at www.llewellyn.com to select your books and place an order on our secure server.

Order by phone:
- • Call toll free within the U.S. at 1-877-NEW-WRLD (1-877-639-9753)
- • Call toll free within Canada at 1-866-NEW-WRLD (1-866-639-9753)
- • We accept VISA, MasterCard, and American Express

Order by mail:
Send the full price of your order (MN residents add 6.875% sales tax) in U.S. funds, plus postage and handling to: Llewellyn Worldwide, 2143 Wooddale Drive Woodbury, MN 55125-2989

POSTAGE AND HANDLING
STANDARD (U.S. & Canada):
(Please allow 12 business days)
$25.00 and under, add $4.00.
$25.01 and over, FREE SHIPPING.
INTERNATIONAL ORDERS (airmail only):
$16.00 for one book, plus $3.00 for each additional book.
Visit us online for more shipping options.
Prices subject to change.

FREE CATALOG!

To order, call
1-877-
NEW-WRLD
ext. 8236
or visit our
website

High Forehead
"Inhidden hit is intelligent
and has an active mind"

Dilated Pupils
"Eyes express interest to each other"

Small Nostrils
"Shows she's cautious"

Sensual Lips
"Mutual interest in one other"

Face Reading
QUICK & EASY
Richard Webster

Face Reading Quick & Easy
RICHARD WEBSTER

Based on ancient Chinese wisdom similar to palmistry and acupuncture, face reading teaches us to really see the faces we look at every day. Learn how the zones of the face reveal personality characteristics, and how meaning is hidden in our features. Includes exercises designed to help you read the fortunes, struggles, and triumphs written on your own face and those of friends, family, colleagues, and business contacts. Also included are helpful tips for reading emotional cues during important meetings like job interviews, and tips for recognizing when a person is lying.

978-0-7387-3296-1, 264 pp., 6 x 9　　　　　　　　　　**$16.99**

To order, call 1-877-NEW-WRLD
Prices subject to change without notice
Order at Llewellyn.com 24 hours a day, 7 days a week!

Aura
Reading

For Beginners

Develop Your Psychic Awareness for Health & Success

RICHARD WEBSTER

Aura Reading for Beginners
Develop Your Psychic Awareness for Health & Success
RICHARD WEBSTER

Fully comprehend those around you by learning to read their aura, the energetic manifestation of the soul. Watch for a dirty red haze around those who have just lost their temper, or an expanded aura for those doing philanthropic deeds. Learn to see auras through the proven methods taught by Richard Webster in his psychic training classes, including exploring the chakra system and learning how to restore balance. Then, begin to imprint your desires into your aura to attract what you want in your life. These proven methods for seeing and reading auras will help you:

—Interpret the meanings of colors in the aura

—Find a career that is best suited for you

—Relate better to the people in your life

—Enjoy excellent health

—Discover areas of your life that you need to work on

—Imprint what you want in your future into your aura

—Discover the signs of impending ill health, drug abuse, and pain

—Change the state of your aura and stimulate specific chakras through music, crystals, and color

978-1-56718-798-4, 208 pp., 5³⁄₁₆ x 8   **$12.95**

To order, call 1-877-NEW-WRLD
Prices subject to change without notice
Order at Llewellyn.com 24 hours a day, 7 days a week!

Color Magic for Beginners
RICHARD WEBSTER

From our clothes to the color of our bedroom walls, we are surrounded by colors that influence our mood, energy level, creativity, and overall well-being. Richard Webster offers an astonishing number of ways to use stimulating reds, soothing blues, and every other color of the rainbow to our advantage.

Webster begins with an overall picture of each color's major aspects—its psychological influence, healing qualities, emotional impact, and magical characteristics. From there, readers learn a multitude of color-based techniques involving astrology, the aura, candle magic, chakras, color rituals, crystals and gemstones, feng shui, flower magic, mandalas, meditation, numerology, and visualization. Webster demonstrates how color can be used to attract good luck, heal illness, reduce stress, create harmony in the home, overcome depression, solve problems, and magically enhance one's life in a variety of ways.

978-0-7387-0886-7, 264 pp., 5³⁄₁₆ x 8   **$13.95**

To order, call 1-877-NEW-WRLD
Prices subject to change without notice
Order at Llewellyn.com 24 hours a day, 7 days a week!

Intuition

For Beginners

Easy Ways to Awaken Your Natural Abilities

DIANE BRANDON

Intuition for Beginners
Easy Ways to Awaken Your Natural Abilities
DIANE BRANDON

Have you ever known who was calling when the phone rang? Or have you ever made a decision on an absolute whim—and later felt that you made the right choice? Perhaps you've had an immediate good or bad feeling about a person—and then had that instinct confirmed? Most people, whether they acknowledge it or not, have some degree of intuitive ability.

Diane Brandon has spent the past two decades studying intuitive development. Whether your intuition is naturally accessible or hidden, this comprehensive and approachable text offers strategies to elevate your level of conscious awareness. Dispelling the myths of intuitive and psychic knowledge, Brandon focuses on how intuition can be applied as a tool of empowerment and self-improvement. Get in touch with your inner voice to improve relationships, solve problems, make well-timed decisions, and more.

978-0-7387-3335-7, 312 pp., 5³⁄₁₆ x 8 $14.99

To order, call 1-877-NEW-WRLD
Prices subject to change without notice
Order at Llewellyn.com 24 hours a day, 7 days a week!

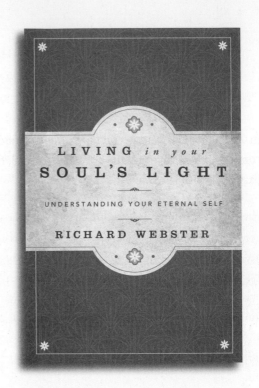

LIVING *in your*
SOUL'S LIGHT

UNDERSTANDING YOUR ETERNAL SELF

RICHARD WEBSTER

Living in Your Soul's Light
Understanding Your Eternal Self
RICHARD WEBSTER

In 2010, popular author Richard Webster had a brush with death that compelled him to write this book on the soul, the spiritual and immortal part of each of us.

Friendly and accessible, this guide explores beliefs and customs regarding the soul, past lives, and reincarnation in cultures all over the world. Webster explains auras, chakras, and soul mates. He discusses the Seven Rays, powerful universal energies that have a profound effect on the soul. Webster reveals how each of the Seven Rays is related to a specific life purpose, and presents quizzes, meditations, and exercises designed to help readers determine their ray and soul purpose for this lifetime.

978-0-7387-3249-7, 264 pp., 5³⁄₁₆ x 8   **$15.95**

To order, call 1-877-NEW-WRLD
Prices subject to change without notice
Order at Llewellyn.com 24 hours a day, 7 days a week!

DJUNA WOJTON

KARMIC CHOICES

HOW MAKING THE RIGHT

DECISIONS CAN CREATE

ENDURING JOY

Karmic Choices
How Making the Right Decisions Can Create Enduring Joy
DJUNA WOJTON

Karmic Choices gives you the tools to get unstuck by designing an exciting, interesting, and productive life. With exercises, questionnaires, and Djuna Wojton's three-step karmic formula, this book will help you:

—Heal old issues and set new goals
—Go beyond self-imposed limitations
—Experience greater productivity
—Get support from friends, family, and professionals
—Create new strategies for lasting joy
—Take actions that positively impact the environment and the world

Release the blocks that keep you immobilized and create a life you love. Develop your intuition and connect with your soul awareness. Open up to more satisfaction in your career, relationships, and in your self-expression. Djuna Wojton's law of karma brings a new perspective to working with the law of attraction to manifest the life you desire.

978-0-7387-3616-7, 312 pp., 5³⁄₁₆ x 8   **$16.99**

To order, call 1-877-NEW-WRLD
Prices subject to change without notice
Order at Llewellyn.com 24 hours a day, 7 days a week!

THE
SERENITY
SOLUTION

How to Use
Quiet Contemplation
to
Solve Life's Problems

KEITH PARK, PHD

The Serenity Solution
How to Use Quiet Contemplation
to Solve Life's Problems
Keith Park, PhD

Gain a greater awareness of self, learn how to solve life problems, and achieve the life conditions you desire. By demonstrating how to employ calm focus—an alert yet relaxed, optimal state of mind—*The Serenity Solution* helps you approach situations with an increased range of thinking and improves your ability to see all options when facing difficulties.

This clear and effective guide utilizes the strategies that great thinkers, meditators, and problem solvers have worked with over the centuries to achieve mindful results. Discover a variety of easy-to-follow concepts, simple illustrations, and step-by-step exercises to help broaden insight. Do away with your negative outlook and bring better health and relationships into full view.

978-0-7387-3678-5, 216 pp., 6 x 9   **$14.99**

To order, call 1-877-NEW-WRLD
Prices subject to change without notice
Order at Llewellyn.com 24 hours a day, 7 days a week!

DISCOVER YOUR
Inner Wisdom
THROUGH
Dowsing

Intuition
in an
Instant

KATHRYN KLVANA

Intuition in an Instant
Discover Your Inner Wisdom Through Dowsing
Kathryn Klvana

Kick-start your intuition with a practical, easy-to-learn skill that will have countless uses in your life. Discover how age-old techniques for finding water can help you get an answer to any question instantly, giving you intuitive guidance on the spot whenever you need it.

Most people prefer to use a small pendulum when asking intuitive questions, rather than the classic forked stick or Y-rod. You'll learn to trust your intuition and make better decisions, remove blocks that are keeping you from achieving your dreams, and become more effective at work. You can use the knowledge gained from dowsing to improve your relationships, enhance your health, even communicate with your pets. Save time, energy, and money by using this simple form of divination.

978-0-7387-2330-3, 240 pp., 5 x 7   **$14.95**

To order, call 1-877-NEW-WRLD
Prices subject to change without notice
Order at Llewellyn.com 24 hours a day, 7 days a week!

153.6
WEB

Webster, Richard.

Body language

DUE DATE   16.99